Resilience:
Adapt and Plan for the New Abnormal of the COVID-19 Coronavirus Pandemic

The *Resilience* Series

Resilience:
Adapt and Plan for the New Abnormal of the COVID-19 Coronavirus Pandemic

Gleb Tsipursky

CHANGEMAKERS
BOOKS

Winchester, UK
Washington, USA

JOHN HUNT PUBLISHING

First published by Changemakers Books, 2020
Changemakers Books is an imprint of John Hunt Publishing Ltd., No. 3 East Street,
Alresford, Hampshire SO24 9EE, UK
office@jhpbooks.com
www.johnhuntpublishing.com
www.changemakers-books.com

For distributor details and how to order please visit the 'Ordering' section on our website.

ISBN: 978 1 78904 675 5
978 1 78904 676 2 (ebook)
Library of Congress Control Number: 00000000

A CIP catalogue record for this book is available from the British Library.

Design: Stuart Davies

UK: Printed and bound by CPI Group (UK) Ltd, Croydon, CR0 4YY
Printed in North America by CPI GPS partners

We operate a distinctive and ethical publishing philosophy in
all areas of our business, from our global network of authors to
production and worldwide distribution.

Contents

Other Books by this Author

(co-written with Tim Ward) Pro Truth: A Practical Plan for Putting Truth Back into Politics (Changemakers Books, 2020)
ISBN-10: 1789043999

The Blindspots Between Us: How to Overcome Unconscious Cognitive Bias & Build Better Relationships (New Harbinger, 2020)
ISBN-10: 1684035082

Never Go With Your Gut: How Pioneering Leaders Make the Best Decisions and Avoid Business Disasters (Career Press, 2019)
ISBN-10: 1632651629

Find Your Purpose Using Science (Intentional Insights, 2015)
ISBN-10: 0-9964692-0-6

The Truth-Seeker's Handbook: A Science-Based Guide (Intentional Insights, 2017)
ISBN-10: 0-9964692-2-2

Book Foreword

Adapt and Plan for the New Abnormal of the COVID-19 Coronavirus Pandemic

The world is in trouble – but, thanks to the wisdom in this book, you don't have to be a victim and sit waiting for some government to help you. You can plan. You can adapt. The decisions you can make in the months to come can help you steer your family, your business, your community, onto a safer path, even while others are driving blindly. Gleb Tsipursky has done a masterful job of pulling together not only the essential tools and strategies for planning your way forward, he also offers a clear-eyed perspective on how our leaders failed to respond when the threat emerged.

Why do I put so much trust in Dr. Tsipursky?

Well, for one thing, he made the right calls on the trajectory of the pandemic long before it was widely recognized as a global crisis. For example, he wrote two articles in late February, in which he critiqued the CDC's advice at that time – which was to plan for a two-week emergency in case of a local outbreak.

In *The Columbus Dispatch* he wrote: "To prepare well for COVID-19, you need to make long-term changes to your life, not simply short-term plans, and accept that we're in a new normal. Instead of a couple of weeks, you should have sufficient supplies for a couple of months in case of quarantines." (https://www.dispatch.com/opinion/20200311/column-one-huge-mistake-to-avoid-in-preparing-for-coronavirus-pandemic)

In *Business Insider*, he wrote: "Forward-looking companies are already encouraging their workers to work remotely as a result of the COVID-19 pandemic. Follow their lead." (https://www.businessinsider.com/disaster-expert-companies-should-face-coronavirus-with-pessimism-2020-3)

Both news outlets waited till March 11th to publish these

articles – perhaps because their editorial departments themselves were cautious about publishing advice so different from what the CDC and other leaders were saying at the time. Indeed, the Editorial Page Editor of *The Columbus Dispatch* later wrote to Dr. Tsipursky in a private e-mail on March 15: "my concern initially was that the column might be a bit too much; now I agree you were very much ahead of the curve and on target."

March 7th the President tweeted: "So last year 37,000 Americans died from the common Flu. It averages between 27,000 and 70,000 per year. Nothing is shut down, life & the economy go on. At this moment there are 546 confirmed cases of CoronaVirus, with 22 deaths. Think about that!" And indeed, many people continued to refer to the gathering epidemic as "just the flu."

It was the same with business leaders. Elon Musk tweeted on March 6 that: "The coronavirus panic is dumb," and on March 19 that: "Based on current trends, probably close to zero new cases in US too by end of April."

Indeed, as late as mid-March very few were predicting the US was on the same trajectory as Italy. As a result of underestimating the threat, we wasted precious weeks while the epidemic spread like wildfire. Looking back, one wonders, how could we have been so blind?

Dr. Tsipursky has no crystal ball; as a behavioral economist and cognitive neuroscientist, his expertise is in recognizing the blindspots in our nature – cognitive biases – that lead us to misperceive reality and make disastrous errors in our decision-making. These errors are costing lives and ruining livelihoods. Please make use of the practical advice he shares in this concise and practical guide. They will help keep you safe, and enable you to plan for your future in "the new abnormal."

Tim Ward
Publisher, Changemakers Books
May 1, 2020

Series Foreword

Resilience In a Time of Crisis

"What can we do to help?"

In a time of crisis – such as the 2020 COVID-19 pandemic – we all have a natural impulse to help our neighbors. John Hunt, founder of John Hunt Publishing, asked this question of our company, and then offered a suggestion. He proposed producing a series of short books written by experts offering practical, emotional, and spiritual skills to help people survive in the midst of a crisis.

To reach people when they need it most, John wanted to accomplish this in forty days. Bear in mind, the normal process of bringing a book from concept to market takes at least eighteen months. As publisher of the JHP imprint Changemakers Books, I volunteered to execute this audacious plan. My imprint publishes books about personal and social transformation, and I already knew many authors with exactly the kinds of expertise we needed. That's how the Resilience Series was born.

I was overwhelmed by my authors' responses. Ten of them immediately said yes and agreed to the impossible deadline. The book you hold in your hands is the result of this intensive, collaborative effort. On behalf of John, myself, the authors and production team, our intention for you is that you take to heart the skills and techniques offered to you in these pages. Master them. Make yourself stronger. Share your newfound resilience with those around you. Together, we can not only survive, but learn how to thrive in tough times. By so doing, we can find our way to a better future.

Tim Ward
Publisher, Changemakers Books
May 1, 2020

Introduction

The COVID-19 pandemic has fundamentally disrupted our professional and personal lives, our businesses and nonprofits, and our society as a whole. We will never go back to the world of January 2020.

To survive and thrive in this new abnormal, you have to make a radical departure from your previous course. Instead, you need to focus on adapting to and planning for a future shaped by the impact and repercussions of the pandemic.

When historians look back to our time, they will rate the winners and losers by how quickly the former pivoted, and how long the latter dawdled. All of us will be judged by how readily we revised our personal lives, professional careers, and the business models of our organizations to succeed in the context of the slow-moving train wreck of the pandemic. This book will guide you to being on the right side of history.

Sounds a bit pessimistic and alarmist? I wish it was! I'd love nothing better than for me to be wrong, for the pandemic to disappear, like a miracle, the day the book is published, and for you to laugh at my silly predictions.

Yet this wish, I very much fear, is in vain, dear reader. We're stuck with the pandemic and its consequences for the next several years. Our realistic – not magical – best-case, most-optimistic scenario for putting COVID-19 to rest is getting most people vaccinated by early 2022. Very likely, it will happen many months and even years after that extremely ambitious date. In the meantime, we'll be suffering rolling waves of outbreaks leading to shutdowns, social distancing, economic disruption, and civil unrest.

Even after widespread vaccination, our society will be changed – forever. How could it be otherwise, when we would have spent so much time cooped up inside our homes, socially distanced from family and friends and co-workers, living our lives and doing our work virtually instead of in-person? Our social norms, habits, desires, and expectations will be different in ways we can hardly imagine right now. So will yours: no matter how certain you may be that on the day after COVID-19 is officially over in your country, you'll spend the whole day giving strangers free hugs (or maybe that's just me), you will very likely have a different perspective in that future moment years from now.

I say all this as an inveterate optimist. No really, it's true: despite what you might see as the gloomy spirit of the book, I feel hope and positivity about the future. Sure, this book might have disturbing and painful information that you don't want to hear about the reality of what we're facing. Heck, I had trouble internalizing this information myself when I first learned it, and I had to overcome deep-seated resistance from my coaching and consulting clients when I conveyed it to them. Still, I'm hopeful that you, dear reader, will be savvy about incorporating into your plans the strategies you need to navigate the new abnormal of the pandemic with minimal losses and maximum gains. Without my optimism, I wouldn't be writing this book; I'd just be hiding under a rock somewhere.

My optimism and passion to help people avoid suffering motivated me to pursue my career as an expert in disaster avoidance, decision-making, risk management, and strategic planning. Since 1999, I have consulted, coached, and trained business and nonprofit leaders in these areas. I also spent over 15 years studying these topics as a cognitive neuroscientist and behavioral economist in academia, earning a PhD at the University of North Carolina at Chapel Hill from 2004 to 2011 and serving as a professor at The Ohio State University from 2011 to 2018, and publishing dozens of peer-reviewed articles in academic journals such as *Behavior and Social Issues* and *Journal of Social and Political Psychology*. Moonlighting during that time as a consultant, coach, trainer, and speaker, I've since gone into private business full-time as CEO of Disaster Avoidance Experts in 2018.

By the time you read these words, I have become an internationally-known thought leader on these topics. My cutting-edge expertise has been featured in over 550 published articles and over 450 interviews I've given to prominent media venues. These include *Inc. Magazine, Fast Company, CBS News, Time, Scientific American, Psychology Today, The Conversation, Business Insider, Government Executive, The Chronicle of Philanthropy, Entrepreneur, CNBC, NPR,* and many others. I also became a best-selling author, best known for my national best-seller, *Never Go With Your Gut: How Pioneering Leaders Make the Best Decisions and Avoid Business Disasters* (Career Press, 2019). It's the first book to focus on cognitive biases in business leadership and reveal how leaders can overcome these dangerous judgment errors effectively. I also wrote *The Truth Seeker's Handbook: A Science-Based Guide* (Intentional Insights, 2017), on facing uncomfortable truths in personal and professional life; *The Blindspots Between Us: How to Overcome Unconscious Cognitive Bias and Build Better Relationships* (New Harbinger, April 2020), the first book to focus on cognitive biases in professional and personal relationships, and illustrate how we can defeat these dangerous judgment errors in our relationships; and, together with Tim Ward, who also kindly wrote the Foreword to the book you're reading, I wrote *Pro Truth: A Practical Plan for Putting Truth Back into Politics* (Changemakers Books, 2020), a primer on how to make truth matter in our politics again and defeat the cognitive biases that plague our political system.

As Tim kindly noted in his Foreword, my expertise and vision – and ability to set aside temporarily my optimism – enabled me to foresee the dangers and impact of COVID-19 long before the top political and business leaders did so, despite the much better sources of information available to them. Having seen my articles on this topic, he invited me to write this book, on an extremely tight timeline. While I was busy helping my existing coaching and consulting clients navigate the early stages of the pandemic, I also felt a great deal of sadness and frustration by seeing so many devastating mistakes by everyone from top business leaders to my neighbors in their deeply inadequate response to COVID-19.

It especially hurt when my 79-year-old dad developed a severe case of COVID-19 in early April after my parents failed to take adequate precautions despite my numerous warnings. To quote Mark 6:4, "A prophet is not without honor, save in his own country, and among his own kin, and in his own house." Fortunately, he recovered with my mom's care, but it was touch and go for a while, and I was really worried, sad, and anxious for a couple of weeks. Now, as this book goes into publication in the end of April, my mom, who is 70 and undergoing breast cancer treatment, has begun coughing and experiencing shortness of breath. I'm very much hoping it's just a cold and that she didn't pick up COVID-19 from my dad.

The book that you're reading is my best effort to help you understand the neuroscience and behavioral economics-based insights on why we respond so poorly to slow-moving, high-impact disasters such as COVID-19, the topic of the first chapter. More importantly, it will help you understand how to adapt to COVID-19 effectively, whether you're a private individual focusing on your household and career, the focus of the second chapter, or a business, nonprofit, or municipal leader concerned with your organization, described in the third chapter. Finally, it will empower you to make an effective strategic plan to survive and thrive through the pandemic and guide you into the post-pandemic society in the fourth and fifth chapters. I suggest you read the book from the beginning, but if you're extremely pressed for time, you can skip to the chapter that most concerns you, and then return to read the book from the start.

I very much hope – in fact, am full of optimism – that reading this book will help you to be on the right side of history when the history books are written. Let's be winners together: please join me in using the most effective research-based strategies to adapt and plan for the new abnormal of the pandemic. I'm excited to hear what you think of this book: as you go through it, and especially as you finish it, e-mail me with any questions and thoughts at Gleb@DisasterAvoidanceExperts.com. More resources from the book, including a workbook, recorded webinar, and updated information about how to adapt and plan most effectively for COVID-19, are available at https://disasteravoidanceexperts.com/adapt.

Chapter 1

Why Do We Make Bad Decisions Around Pandemics Such as COVID-19?

"We have it under control. It's going to be just fine." That's what US President Donald Trump said about *severe acute respiratory syndrome coronavirus 2 (SARS-CoV-2)*, the coronavirus that causes the COVID-19 disease, in a January 22, 2020 interview on CNBC's "Squawk Box." During a Fox News interview on February 10, Trump shared that: "I really believe they are going to have it under control fairly soon. You know in April, supposedly, it dies with the hotter weather." On March 13, Patrick Vallance, chief scientific advisor to the UK government, in an interview for BBC Radio, said that the government aims to "build up some kind of herd immunity so more people are immune to this disease and we reduce the transmission." The president of the European Commission Ursula von der Leyen said in a March 19 interview for *Bild*, "I think that all of us who are not experts initially underestimated the coronavirus."

The prominent businessman Elon Musk, founder of Tesla and SpaceX, tweeted on March 6 that, "The coronavirus panic is dumb," and on March 19 that: "Based on current trends, probably close to zero new cases in US too by end of April." On January 28, Hartmut Issel, UBS Global Wealth Management Head of Equity and Credit, told CNBC that COVID-19 will not have much of an impact beyond decreasing somewhat China's economic production in the first quarter of 2020. Goldman Sachs, in a research note to clients publicized by CNBC on February 19, warned that COVID-19 will likely lead to a near-term fall in stock prices, but will be unlikely to result in a major problem such as a bear market.

Naturally, the large majority of the population in the US and

Europe followed the guidance of their political and business leaders, giving short shrift to the threat posed by the novel coronavirus.

What gives? Why did top political and business leaders, in the US and Europe alike, underestimate the COVID-19 coronavirus pandemic?

It's not like doing so had personal political benefits for the political leaders. They wound up thoroughly humiliated when they had to reverse their rhetoric and policies dismissing the problem, thus hurting their political ratings. And of course, much more seriously, their behavior led to many more people getting sick and dying than should have been the case, if they had made the right decisions.

Neither did business leaders win out in denying the reality of COVID-19. Those like Musk who failed to prepare, adapt, and plan ahead for the pandemic lost their companies a lot of money. Investors unprepared for the impact of the pandemic on the markets suffered a major hit to their portfolios.

The causes stem from a combination of three factors: the nature of the virus itself, the preexisting beliefs and plans of the political and business leaders, and the dangerous judgment errors we all tend to make, errors that neuroscientists and behavioral economists call *cognitive biases*.

Cognitive Biases and the Coronavirus

So what are cognitive biases? Many pundits heap praise on business leaders who make quick gut decisions: about the direction of their company, about whether to launch a new product, about which candidate to hire. Sadly, just going with our gut frequently leads to devastating results for our professional and personal lives.

Consider the Equifax data breach scandal. In May 2017, hackers stole the credit information of over 148 million people from the consumer credit reporting company Equifax, exploiting a security flaw that the company should have known it needed to fix. Indeed, a December 2018 Congressional Report by the House Oversight Committee called the data breach "entirely preventable."

Even worse, the Equifax C-suite decided to cover up the incident for several months. The disastrous decision to conduct a cover-up – inevitably discovered later – gravely damaged Equifax's reputation, caused a large and lasting drop in the company's stock, and led to the CEO and a number of other top executives being forced out due to incompetence.

What about the Boeing leadership's catastrophic decision-making on rushing its 737 Max airplane into production, despite a number of safety issues well known inside the company? In fact, one Boeing pilot in a message to a colleague in 2016 said, "this airplane is designed by clowns, who in turn are supervised by monkeys."

Undeterred by such concerns inside the company, the Boeing leadership went ahead with production, cutting corners in the approval process. The story ends with two deadly crashes that killed 346 people and grounded the 737 Max, Boeing losing over $25 billion in market value before the pandemic, and the Boeing board firing its CEO.

Make no mistake: each of the cases above exemplify value-destroying decisions that hurt shareholders by top corporate leaders who followed their gut. These examples of top leaders at prominent companies are not an isolated instance: a four-year study by LeadershipIQ.com interviewed 1,087 board members from 286 organizations of all sorts that forced out their chief executive officers. It found that over 20% of CEOs got fired for denying reality, meaning they refused to recognize negative facts about the organization's performance. Other research shows that professionals at all levels suffer from the tendency to deny uncomfortable facts in business settings.

Of course, such mental blindspots harm our private lives as

well. We determine our romantic partners by our gut feelings, believing that "the one" will cause us to experience butterflies in our stomach. We pick friends based on our intuitions, choosing the ones with whom we click with instantly and have easy and comfortable conversations. We choose our churches or secular groups, and other forms of community belonging, by what our intuitions tell us about others in that community. We determine who deserves our votes and campaign contributions through considering how we feel about the political candidates in each race, such as through the famous "beer test": with which candidate would you rather have a beer?

Sadly, just going with our gut frequently leads to devastating results for our relationships. It's an often-cited statistic that over 40% of marriages end up in divorce. Trusting our intuitions by going with the person who makes us experience that fluttery sensation upon first meeting is a major contributor to this terribly high rate, since studies show that our first impressions are often wrong. We have many unnecessary fights with friends that lead to hurt feelings and friendship breakups due to miscommunications and misunderstandings resulting from gut responses to what our friends shared. Let's not even speak of what happens when voters choose the folks they would rather have a beer with over one who would formulate the best policy for our country.

Roughly speaking, we have two thinking systems. Daniel Kahneman, who won the Nobel Prize for his research on behavioral economics, calls them System 1 and 2. I prefer the terms autopilot system and intentional system, which I believe describe these systems more clearly.

The autopilot system corresponds to our emotions and intuitions, and its cognitive processes center around the amygdala, an older part of our brain. This system guides our daily habits, helps us make snap decisions, and reacts instantly to dangerous life-and-death situations through the freeze, fight, or flight stress response. While the snap judgments resulting from intuitions and emotions usually feel "true" because they are fast and powerful, they sometimes lead us wrong in systematic and predictable ways.

The intentional system reflects our rational thinking, and centers around the prefrontal cortex, the part of the brain that evolved more recently. This thinking system helps us handle more complex mental activities, such as managing individual and group relationships, logical reasoning, probabilistic thinking, and learning new information and patterns of thinking and behavior.

While the automatic system requires no conscious effort to function, the intentional system takes deliberate effort to turn on and is mentally tiring. Fortunately, with enough motivation and appropriate training, we can learn to use the intentional system to address situations where we tend to make systematic and predictable errors.

Scientists call these mental blindspots cognitive biases. Many of them proved beneficial for our survival in the ancestral savanna environment, when we lived as hunter-gatherers in small tribes, and our ability to survive and reproduce depended on fast instinctive responses much more than reflective analysis.

For example, our primary threat response, which stems from the ancient savanna environment, is the fight-or-flight response, also known as the saber-tooth tiger response. In that environment, it was better for our survival to jump at a hundred shadows than fail to jump at one saber-toothed tiger. A great fit for the kind of short-term intense risks we faced as hunter-gatherers, the fight-or-flight is a much worse fit for the modern world.

You might notice that we have many fewer saber-toothed tigers nowadays. Our main threats come in the form of notifications on our smartphones. Yet, we react to such threats with outsized responses more appropriate to the tigers.

Most of these errors arise from the autopilot system, while others come from the intentional system gone awry. They number in the hundreds, with more being discovered all the time. Fair warning: given that this research is on the cutting edge, some of what you read may later need to be revised as science progresses.

Fortunately, research on the practice of *debiasing* has shown how to overcome these dangerous judgment errors. By learning about how these errors led to bad decisions around the pandemic – by political and business leaders, and ordinary people – in the rest of this chapter, you will start on the path to defeating cognitive biases. You will complete your journey in the following chapters, which go in-depth into the specific techniques for debiasing to adapt and plan most effectively for the pandemic and post-pandemic society. And if you want to learn more about debiasing cognitive biases in professional settings, see my best-selling book *Never Go With Your Gut: How Pioneering Leaders Make the Best Decisions and Avoid Business Disasters*.

Normalcy Bias

The *normalcy bias* refers to the fact that our autopilot system drives us to feel that the future, at least in the short and medium term of the next couple of years, will function in roughly the same way as the past: normally. As a result, we tend to vastly underestimate both the possibility and impact of a disaster striking us.

This bias leads individuals, businesses, and governments to fail to prepare nearly as well as they should for the likelihood and effects of catastrophes, especially slow-moving train wrecks such as pandemics. Moreover, in the midst of the event itself, people react much slower than they ideally should, getting stuck in the mode of gathering information instead of deciding and acting.

It's not surprising that going with our gut reactions leads us astray in response to disasters that slowly gather steam while they approach us. Our threat response causes us, based on our personalities and predispositions, to go into fight-or-flight mode. The fight response causes us to take immediate actions that we perceive as solving the problem, such as buying toilet paper and guns, as so many did in response to COVID-19.

Others fall into the flight response. That might mean flight into themselves, where they essentially freeze by ignoring the information, as so many did in Europe and the US. It might also mean actual flight, where they try to leave their area for one perceived as safer, which many did as well.

Of course, neither of these is the right response for the situation at hand. Fleeing an area or stocking up is fine for the typical disasters that strike a region, such as a hurricane that might cause major flooding as happened in Houston in September 2019. It's not a good fit for the COVID-19 pandemic.

Businesses and nonprofits generally react better than individuals, due to their business continuity plans (full disclosure: preparing such plans is one of my frequent areas of consulting work as a disaster avoidance expert). These plans aim to overcome the typical tendency to underprepare for and react badly in disasters by having a default plan of action. That includes working offsite if there's a fire in the headquarters or having employees cross-trained to cover each other's responsibilities if several key employees get hit by the proverbial bus. Yet their typical continuity plans don't fit the reality of the pandemic (and I had to act quickly to help my clients realize that and revise their plans).

Why not? To understand that requires grasping the nature of COVID-19. A note of caution: given that the novel coronavirus that causes COVID-19 is new, the scientific evidence is constantly evolving to grow more accurate over time. What I cite below is the best evidence available as of the time the book is published, and you can see updated estimates at https://

disasteravoidanceexperts.com/adapt.

The novel coronavirus is highly infectious and we lack immunity to it. As a result, each person who gets sick can take up to two weeks to show symptoms, and about half of all people who get sick are asymptomatic but infectious carriers. Consequently, each infected person can infect 2-3 others with the infection doubling every 3-6 days in any outbreak that's not suppressed.

Early hopes that COVID-19 would disappear by summer have faded. It's spreading in warm weather, even if the spread seems slower than in cold weather.

Current best estimates suggest about 5-10% of those infected with the novel coronavirus require hospital care, and .5-1% die, even with good hospital care. The hospitalization and death rates are much higher for those older or younger people with health issues, such as autoimmune diseases, diabetes, or smoking.

The rapid growth of outbreaks, combined with the lack of hospital capacity, results in medical systems quickly becoming overwhelmed if governments don't take measures to control an outbreak. In those cases, death rates balloon to 5-10% – essentially those who require hospitalization – and much higher for those more vulnerable.

We know that government measures to suppress COVID-19 by shutting down businesses, restricting travel, and directing citizens to stay at home are indeed effective at preventing transmission and reducing new cases. When instituted early enough, they have successfully prevented medical systems from becoming overwhelmed, such as in South Korea, Taiwan, Singapore, and US states such as Ohio.

In other cases, when governments made the bad decision to delay instituting shutdowns – such as in Italy, Spain, and the US state of New York – medical systems became overwhelmed and patients died who shouldn't have died. Yet the eventual delayed shutdowns did bring the case load down sufficiently that hospitals proved eventually able to cope, once the number of critically ill patients decreased.

Yet the Asian countries that successfully suppressed early outbreaks – South Korea, Taiwan, Singapore – all faced a secondary outbreak of COVID-19 after they began to lift restrictions. To control such outbreaks, they had to impose restrictions once again. Indeed, researchers studying how COVID-19 will progress suggest that we'll see similar developments in Europe and the US: loosening of restrictions, followed by outbreaks, followed by more restrictions for a while. We are not getting back to the state of things in January 2020.

Given all that, the only way to deal with COVID-19 conclusively involves finding a vaccine. It usually takes a decade or more to develop a vaccine, due to the extensive financial costs and safety regulations around the approval process. Fortunately, government, market, and philanthropic forces have combined to channel extensive funding toward developing vaccines and minimizing the approval process standards to the bare minimum needed to ensure safety.

Still, while over a hundred organizations launched projects to develop vaccines, and several have created a viable prototype, it will take many months for the vaccine to go through human trials. First, we'll have a trial lasting several months to evaluate whether the vaccine has unacceptable side effects (in a regular, non-emergency situation, this part usually takes 1-2 years). Then, we'll need more trials lasting a few more months to test whether the vaccine is actually effective (typically 2-4 years). Then, government bodies have to review the trial data to confirm effectiveness, which would take another few months (usually 2-4 years). Finally, we'll need to see which of the many vaccines being developed and put through trials offers the best combination of maximal effectiveness with minimal side effects.

According to the top vaccine experts, this is the one step of the process that can't be rushed or solved by throwing money or expertise at it. If we'll be pumping something into the arms of billions of people around the world, we need to get it right.

Now, if a vaccine shows a great deal of promise, it's possible that those at highest risk and most impact, such as medical workers in areas with inadequate protective equipment, might get a vaccine as an experimental measure. For them, the risk might be worth it; besides, their medical training would help ensure that they can give truly informed consent. But that's not mass vaccination.

In the ideal scenario, if one of the first several vaccines does successfully make it through the trials and proves highly effective without any unacceptable side effects – a very big if – we might have a vaccine approved for widespread use by summer of 2021.

What then? Well, we need to manufacture the vaccine in mass, to vaccinate at least the more vulnerable categories and eventually everyone. Producing enough vaccine for only, say, the 100 million vulnerable Americans would take a few months. You also have the obstacle of distributing it and actually vaccinating people, as well as dealing with anti-vaxxer sentiments, so another few months. That brings us into early 2022 on the most optimistic timeline.

Given that only a very small percentage of all vaccines make it through the trials, due either to unacceptable side effects or insufficient effectiveness, we shouldn't expect that we'll get so wonderfully lucky. More realistically, it might not be until 2024-25 when we get a sufficiently safe and effective vaccine.

And if the universe decides to show us the middle finger, we might never find an effective vaccine to COVID-19. After all, we don't have a fully effective vaccine against the flu. The one we have is a weak vaccine, only about 50% effective on average in reducing the likelihood of getting the flu, as well as reducing the severity of the flu if you do get it.

Now, this information was known at least as early as February 2020. However, the normalcy bias makes it very difficult for us to imagine that our world can turn upside down so quickly. In early 2020, it was extremely uncomfortable for political and business leaders, and ordinary citizens, to even begin to imagine that it would take at least until early 2022 before we could – with incredible luck – expect to deal with COVID-19; more realistically 2024-25. That, despite clear statements from the best scientific experts to that effect.

Consider that on March 2, in a rally in Charleston, SC, Trump said, "Today we met with the big great pharmaceutical companies… and they're going to have vaccines, I think relatively soon." On March 24, in a Fox News town hall, as the number of infections and deaths in the US was growing quickly on a clear upward trajectory, Trump said he wanted the US "opened up and just raring to go by Easter," before backing down and proclaiming a continuation of suggested restrictions – though not a full national shutdown – through April. In turn, under intense pressure from all sides for lack of effective suppression that threatened to overwhelm the UK health system, Boris Johnson ordered a national shutdown on March 23.

Think that savvy business leaders whose job it is to evaluate economic developments had a different perspective? Think again.

On February 24, Goldman Sachs cut its forecast for US GDP growth from 2.1% to 1.2% in the first quarter of 2020 due to COVID-19, with the second-quarter GDP growing at 2.7%. That happened when Italy already had a few towns under quarantine from February 23. Italy announced a full national lockdown on March 9. On March 15, when US coronavirus cases took off with developments fully predictable based on the comparable model of Italy, Goldman Sachs now reduced its estimate of US second-quarter GDP to a decline of 5%. Just five days later, Goldman Sachs updated its forecast to a second-quarter decline of 24%.

Clearly, Goldman Sachs screwed up its analysis. Their estimates reflect the sentiments of other major business leaders.

Ordinary people naturally followed the guidance of political and business leaders, and failed to appreciate the depth and magnitude of the pandemic's impact.

Attentional Bias

While the normalcy bias is the most harmful cognitive bias from which we suffer in the face of the pandemic, it's far from the only one. In fact, a number of other cognitive biases combined with normalcy bias to lead to bad decisions about the pandemic.

One of these, *attentional bias*, refers to our tendency to pay attention to information that we find most emotionally engaging, and ignore information that we don't. Given the intense, in-the-moment nature of threats and opportunities in the ancestral savanna, this bias is understandable. Yet in the modern environment, sometimes information that doesn't feel emotionally salient is actually really important.

For example, the fact that the novel coronavirus originated in Wuhan, China, and caused massive sickness and deaths there, didn't draw much attention as a salient potential threat among Europeans and Americans. It proved too easy to dismiss the importance of the outbreak in Wuhan, due to stereotypical and inaccurate visions of the Chinese heartland as full of backwoods peasants.

In reality, Wuhan is a global metropolis. The largest city in central China, it has over 11 million people and produced over $22.5 billion in 2018. It has a good healthcare system, strengthened substantially by China after the SARS pandemic. A major travel hub, Wuhan's nickname is "the Chicago of China"; it had over 500 international flights per day before the outbreak. If we assume an average of 250 people per plane, that's 10,000 people a day flying out of Wuhan to the world.

Europeans and Americans, with the exception of a small number of experts, failed to perceive the threat to themselves from the breakdown of Wuhan's solid healthcare system as it became overwhelmed by COVID-19. They arrogantly assumed this breakdown pointed to the backwardness of China's heartland, rather than the accurate perception that any modern medical system would become overwhelmed in the face of the novel coronavirus.

They also failed to recognize the thorough interconnectedness of Wuhan to the rest of the globe. A case in point: one of the early cases of COVID-19 in the US was diagnosed in a traveler from Wuhan in the state of Washington. The first epicenter of COVID-19 in Europe, Northern Italy, has unusually close ties to Wuhan.

Europeans only began paying serious attention to COVID-19 when it began to take root in Italy. Americans, in turn, started to pay attention when COVID-19 surfaced in Washington state.

Do you know who didn't ignore Wuhan, besides a small number of experts? Those to whom this city felt emotionally salient. Those who understood that Wuhan could be fairly compared to Chicago in the US, Manchester in the UK, or Frankfurt in Germany.

That emotional salience helps explain why many Chinese communities in Europe and America acted quickly and effectively to minimize the impact of COVID-19. For instance, the 50,000 Chinese in Pareto, Italy – a quarter of the city's residents – went into voluntary lockdown at the end of January. That's three weeks before the first recorded infection in Italy.

With their connections to China, they could envision what was to come, and spread the word to close their businesses, stay home as much as possible, and wear masks in the rare cases when venturing outside. That helps explain why, according to Renzo Berti, the top state health official for the region, none of the Chinese residents in Pareto got COVID-19 and the town's infection rate was half of the Italian average, 62 cases per 100,000 people rather than 115 for the entire country.

Imagine what would have happened if everyone behaved like

these ethnic Chinese? Businesses, individuals, and governments acting together could have prevented the enormous death toll and economic devastation from the novel coronavirus. Yet our attentional bias led us astray.

Anchoring

We tend to be too strongly anchored by the initial information we have and fail to update our beliefs sufficiently based on new evidence, even if this evidence is, objectively speaking, much more persuasive. This dangerous judgment error, called *anchoring*, harmed us in two profound ways with COVID-19.

First, business and political leaders and ordinary people anchored on past pandemics within living memory, which – while serious – didn't cause widespread disruption. SARS, the first pandemic of the 21st century, led to around 750 deaths in 26 countries. The H1N1, also known as the swine flu, killed many more, as many as half a million. Yet it didn't impact the US too much, with about 12,500 deaths, and even less in the UK, at about 500, which was at the high end of deaths in Europe. Ebola and Zika barely reached Europe or the US. As a result, the large majority of Americans and Europeans ignored COVID-19, thinking it would pass them by as did these other illnesses.

The second profound harm came from the comparisons of COVID-19 to the flu. In a March 4 interview on Fox News, Donald Trump called COVID-19 the "corona flu" and said the death rate "is way under 1%," implying it's nothing to worry about and that we don't need to take major actions to address the situation. He affirmed this in a March 9 tweet: "last year 37,000 Americans died from the common flu. It averages between 27,000 and 70,000 per year. Nothing is shut down, life & the economy go on."

Other leaders conveyed similar messages that everything is normal. For example, on March 5, with 116 diagnosed cases of COVID-19 and the first death in the UK, Boris Johnson said it's "business as usual." Despite wide criticism and the glaring example of Italy, Johnson's administration failed to impose lockdowns. Instead, it advised in early March that people simply wash their hands, and, if they recently went to Northern Italy and showed flu-like symptoms, to self-isolate for 14 days. On March 11, with 590 confirmed cases, David Halpern, chief executive of the government's Behavioural Insights Team, told BBC News that the government's aim involved shielding the most vulnerable people. The government would allow COVID-19 to infect the UK population more broadly until the population developed herd immunity such that COVID-19 would stop transmitting itself, which requires about 60% to be infected. Next day, at a press conference, Johnson confirmed this strategy, telling people with flu-like symptoms to self-isolate and people over 70 to avoid cruises.

Indeed, the estimated fatality rate from COVID-19, about .5-1% with good-quality treatment, is much lower than the 50% average for Ebola and the 15% for SARS. Yet the infection rate is much higher, in part because about half of all who get infected don't show any symptoms and even those who eventually show symptoms are often infectious before they do. As a result, without strict controls, every infected person gets 2-3 others sick and any outbreak doubles in 3-6 days. Furthermore, about 10-20% of those infected have a serious illness, mainly older adults, and about half of those with a serious illness need to go to the hospital. Given the fact that hospitals have low capacity for a surge of patients, a major outbreak would overwhelm healthcare systems, as happened in Wuhan and Northern Italy by the time of Trump and Johnson's statements.

Their irresponsible approach set the anchor for the approach of most other political and business leaders and ordinary citizens in their respective countries. Such anchoring cost many lives and untold billions of dollars and pounds.

Hyperbolic Discounting

In the savanna environment, our ancestors had to live in and for the moment, since they couldn't effectively invest resources to improve their future states (it's not like they could freeze the meat of the mammoths they killed). Right now, we have many ways of investing into our future lives, such as saving money in banks. Yet our instincts always drive us to orient toward short-term rewards and sacrifice our long-term future, a mental blindspot called *hyperbolic discounting*.

That's why leaders across Europe and the US, political and business alike, largely failed to act in a timely manner to address COVID-19, as Ursula von der Leyen acknowledged. Despite extensive evidence showing that any outbreak grew exponentially, both Boris Johnson and Donald Trump rejected calls in the early stages of outbreaks to take the course of action shown to be effective elsewhere. They did not impose shutdowns and social distancing, along with thorough testing, contact tracing, and isolation.

Following their examples, business leaders largely proceeded with business as usual. Only a few, such as Twitter, Square, and Google, led the way in encouraging employees to work from home, while the English Premier League led the way in cancelling matches.

These political and business leaders felt in their gut that the short-term sacrifices of the shutdowns would not outweigh the long-term benefits of decreasing the impact of the pandemic. It took enormous efforts to convince them otherwise.

Johnson and Trump only began to shift when an impactful report published by researchers from Imperial College London on March 17 suggested that continuing on their current path would result in over 500,000 deaths in the UK and over 2,000,000 in the US. The report demonstrated convincingly that the seemingly low death rate from COVID-19 when treated appropriately hid the much larger death rate that would occur in the UK and US if healthcare systems became overwhelmed.

Doing nothing would result in a sharp surge of cases, disastrously overwhelming the hospitals in both countries. Thus, the death rate would shoot up an order of magnitude, from .5-1% to 5-10%. What kind of an economy and social life can you have with people dying like flies?

Fortunately, both Trump and Johnson called for more strict shutdowns the day the report was published. For example, Trump at a news conference that day said, "We're asking everyone to work at home, if possible, postpone unnecessary travel, and limit social gatherings to no more than 10 people" for the next two weeks. Yet if they had paid actual attention to Wuhan, they wouldn't have taken actions that resulted in so many deaths and so many trillions of dollars lost in both countries by taking steps early to limit the spread and impact of COVID-19.

Planning Fallacy

We tend to feel optimistic about our plans: we made them, and therefore the plans must be good, right? We intuitively feel that our plans will go according to plan, failing to prepare nearly adequately enough for threats and risks. As a result, our initial plans often don't work out, and we either fail to accomplish our goals or require much more time, money, and other resources to get where we wanted to go originally, a cognitive bias known as the *planning fallacy*.

The UK relied way too much on its existing pandemic plan of getting herd immunity for illnesses with low death rates. The Johnson administration failed to account for the lack of hospital surge capacity and protective equipment.

The Trump administration lacked a plan altogether. It disbanded in 2018 the National Security Council directorate at the White House tasked with preparing for the next pandemic. It also cut funding for pandemic preparedness, such as eliminating the $30,000,000 Complex Crisis Fund, and repeatedly pushing for major budget cuts to the Centers for Disease Control and Prevention (CDC). When CDC experts rang the alarm about the coming pandemic in January 2020, the Trump administration ignored them.

After very belatedly acknowledging the threat of COVID-19, Trump refused to take responsibility for fighting it. Instead, at a March 19 press conference, he called on the governors of each state to procure needed supplies instead of the federal government taking on the responsibility as elsewhere around the globe, saying that "we're not a shipping clerk."

The result? A chaos of competing bids and price gouging for ventilators and protective equipment.

The Trump administration let maintenance contracts lapse in 2018 for the federal Strategic National Stockpile of medical equipment, leading to breakage when they were needed most. It also failed to address the clear upcoming need for medical equipment in a timely manner, making its first order for 500 million N95 masks on March 4.

Likewise, the Trump administration experienced a dramatic planning fallacy on COVID-19 testing. While COVID-19 was discovered in South Korea and the US on the same day, by March 6 the US had tested under 2,000 people, but South Korea had tested over 140,000.

Keep in mind, a study in late 2019 by the Nuclear Threat Initiative (NTI) and the Johns Hopkins Center for Health Security (JHCHS) rated the US as the country best prepared for a pandemic. Yet the administration's incompetent response resulted in one of the worst responses among developed countries.

The official US and UK government advice for ordinary people, businesses, nonprofits, and other organizations to plan for the pandemic in early and mid-March followed the unrealistically optimistic perspectives of the Trump and Johnson administrations. The guidance only started to shift following the Imperial College London study on March 17. For instance, the

CDC guidelines in the US in early and mid-March suggested that individuals and households:

- Prepare for being out of commission for 2 weeks if they get sick
- Stock up on daily consumables, such as food, medications, and cleaning supplies, for a couple of weeks in case they get sick
- Wash their hands frequently for 20 seconds
- Prepare for possibly working from home and/or that schools might temporarily close in case of local outbreaks
- Coordinate with your neighbors to help each other
- Get ready for the psychological impact of the situation

Advice for companies and nonprofits included:

- Cross-train employees in case some key ones get sick
- Prepare for event cancellations
- Encourage sick employees to stay home
- Perform additional cleaning
- Make a disease outbreak response plan in case there's an outbreak in your area

All of these preparations are for disruptions that might last for a couple of weeks at most resulting from a local outbreak. Indeed, Dr. Anthony Fauci, the Director of the National Institute of Allergy and Infectious Diseases (NIAID), said in a Fox News interview on February 25 that you "don't need to do anything different today than you did yesterday," except think about what you would do in case of community spread. On March 9, Trump tweeted that, "The Fake News Media and their partner, the Democrat Party, is doing everything within its semi-considerable power (it used to be greater!) to inflame the CoronaVirus situation, far beyond what the facts would warrant. Surgeon General, 'The risk is low to the average American.'"

To me, the clear and glaring example of Wuhan and Northern Italy – areas just as developed as anywhere in the world – meant that the same outcomes likely would occur at least in some areas of the US and UK. I wrote a series of articles in early March, for example, in an op-ed published in *The Columbus Dispatch* on March 11, "The current guidance is extremely optimistic. It assumes you might at worst face a one-time, short-term disruption of a couple of weeks. But you shouldn't anticipate such a wildly optimistic scenario. Instead, you need to prepare for a realistic pessimistic scenario," of major disruptions lasting for several years until the development and wide distribution of an effective vaccine.

Unfortunately, the large majority of ordinary people and businesses alike failed to prepare for the reality of the situation to come. In fact, most didn't even follow the patently inadequate official suggestions. For example, a USC Dornsife poll of 2,436 Americans conducted March 10-12 showed that only 22% started to stockpile food, as the administration's guidance still vastly downplayed the problems from the novel coronavirus.

Less than a month later, on April 4, the White House coronavirus response coordinator Dr. Deborah Birx told Americans that "the next 2 weeks are extraordinarily important," and that "this is the moment to not be going to the grocery store, not going to the pharmacy." Easily predictable from developments elsewhere and what we know about the nature of the virus, this dramatic plea would have been much better received if the administration had prepared Americans better or if Americans had evaluated the risks more effectively in spite of the administration's poor guidance.

What about businesses and other organizations? The large majority either trusted the government's guidelines of preparing for potential short-term local outbreaks or, even worse, dismissed the possible impact of COVID-19 altogether due to anchoring around previous pandemics.

The ones who actually paid attention dusted off their existing disaster preparedness and business continuity plans. These aim to prepare businesses for the typical short-term emergency: major snowstorm, power outage, fire, flooding, and so on. Leaders just penciled in "cleaning" and "encouraging sick employees to stay home" to the existing plans.

Of course, the existing plans did not offer a good fit for the COVID-19 pandemic. These business continuity plans envisioned protecting organizations from disruptions during an event such as the Hurricane Harvey flooding of Houston. This major disaster caused $125,000,000 in damage and killed 107 people altogether, including 14 in Houston, before the floodwaters dissipated.

Almost no one prepared for anything worse than that for their organization. Yet what they should have prepared for was Houston being flooded, and then staying flooded. The existing plans were like trying to protect yourself from a tsunami with an umbrella.

Unlike the week-long disruption suffered by most Houston-area businesses, the disruption from the pandemic will last, in the best-case scenario, through early 2022. However, no smart disaster preparedness and business continuity plan assumes a best-case scenario. These plans should have oriented toward the realistic pessimistic scenario of 2025 or longer. These failures, while understandable in the context of government guidelines, seriously hurt bottom lines and led to a lot of avoidable economic pain, for shareholders and employees alike.

In the next chapter, we'll explore how you can adapt to COVID-19 effectively as an individual focusing on your household and career. Remember, get many more resources from the book, including a workbook, recorded webinar, and up-to-date content about adapting and planning for COVID-19 based on the latest research, at https://disasteravoidanceexperts. com/adapt.

Chapter 2

How to Adapt to the New Abnormal of COVID-19: Individuals, Households, and Careers

So now you know what went wrong in making decisions around COVID-19 for political and business leaders, as well as for individuals and households. What can we do to adapt effectively to the reality of the situation, from the perspective of individuals concerned with their households and careers?

First and foremost, we won't get anywhere if we don't face the facts. We need to acknowledge that COVID-19 fundamentally disrupted our world, turning it upside down in a few short weeks in February and March 2020. We have to move past the discomfort of the normalcy bias and our intuitive feeling that the novel coronavirus "one day, it's like a miracle, it will disappear," to quote Donald Trump's words from a February 28 press conference.

Regrettably, it will not disappear; believing that it will helped get us mired so deep in this mess, making the US outbreak the worst in the world by early April in terms of the number of deaths, and the UK outbreak one of the worst, due to the fact that the policy in these countries shifted only after the March 17 Imperial College Report.

Instead, we need to adapt to the long haul of battling COVID-19, at least until we create an effective vaccine, mass produce and distribute it, and actually vaccinate people. Very optimistically, as the previous chapter outlined, that will be in early 2022; more realistically, 2024-25; pessimistically, we'd never get an effective vaccine, for instance making do with weak versions that prevent 50% of all infections, as we have with the flu.

Prior to a vaccine, we will be coping with COVID-19 through extreme measures such as thorough lockdowns and extensive social distancing in areas with outbreaks that don't have the capacity and/or the political will to do the public health work that enables less extraordinary measures. That public health work involves not only providing the equipment, medications, and personnel needed to treat a surge of patients during outbreaks: that's necessary, but not sufficient.

To relax extreme measures requires the public health work of quickly testing those with flu-like symptoms, isolating anyone who tests positive for COVID-19, contact tracing anyone they interacted with and asking those people to self-quarantine for two weeks, and using antibody testing to certify those who recovered from COVID-19 and are at least temporarily protected from reinfection to work in exposed areas. It also requires public education work of getting people to comply with social distancing, wear masks, minimize unnecessary social contacts, impose social peer pressure on noncompliers, and more broadly follow public health guidelines and support health workers.

These techniques worked effectively for Taiwan, South Korea, Singapore, and other Asian countries that largely managed to avoid the shutdowns in North America and Europe. Likewise, European countries that followed these strategies experienced much less damage, in lives and dollars, due to COVID-19. For instance, while COVID-19 was detected earlier in Germany than Italy (January 28 vs. January 30), Germany's public health system pursued the public health and education campaigns followed by Asian countries. As a result, by April 9, Germany had 2,349 deaths due to COVID-19, while Italy had 17,669, the US had 17,669, and the UK had 7,097, according to Statista.com.

It appears that the US and UK federal governments don't have the political will to pursue the public health and education strategy. Thus, unless you live in an area with an unusually proactive and well-funded regional government that pursues this strategy, any outbreaks will be dealt with using extreme measures.

Given that reality, you can anticipate that what will happen will be as follows:

1. Extreme lockdowns and social distancing to bring COVID-19 under control in a given area;
2. In a few weeks, a gradual loosening of some restrictions after COVID-19 cases fall to a minimal number;
3. After a few weeks or – if you're lucky – several months, COVID-19 cases will start to grow and the regional government will impose another round of extreme measures.

Such whack-a-mole waves of loosening and tightening restrictions will continue until we find a vaccine, or until the US and UK federal governments are pushed into implementing policies modeled on successful Asian examples.

So how can you most effectively adapt to the uncertainty and dislocation that accompanies this new abnormal?

Adapting for Households, Individuals, and Careers

While you're in a new abnormal, your underlying needs and wants remain the same. You just need to figure out different ways toward satisfying them. These ways should rely much less on interacting in-person with people who aren't part of your immediate household and much more with those who are; they should also rely much less on travel, whether in your local area or around the globe, and much more on staying at home.

You might have heard of Abraham Maslow's theory of human motivation and the pyramid of needs based on his work. More recent research, summarized in Scott Barry Kaufman's excellent book *Transcend: The New Science of Self-Actualization*, revises this model to show that our fundamental needs consist of safety, connection, and self-esteem, and we will feel deprived without them. We also have needs that help us achieve our full potential through personal growth, what Maslow called "self-actualization" and what Kaufman more clearly defined as exploration, love, and purpose. A good approach to adapting to the new abnormal is evaluating your life through the lens of these needs and ensuring that you can still satisfy them.

Safety

Let's start with physical safety. You should make sure you are able to stay safe in your home for up to two months in case of a major outbreak in your area, let's say as bad as what happened in New York City. While unlikely, it pays to prepare for a realistic pessimistic scenario. That means having two months of basic food and cleaning supplies, along with any necessary medications.

To prevent supply disruptions for others, consider buying such goods in bulk from specialized online vendors rather than emptying the shelves in your local grocery store. It's both more responsible and cheaper.

Having these consumables will also provide protection in case a member of your household develops a serious case of COVID-19. It might take up to two months for the person who got sick to get better, and of course you would need to stay quarantined during that period. Given that online grocery delivery might not be available – I know I had trouble ordering basic groceries due to high demand for online delivery – having those basic necessities on hand is critically important. Notice that two months is much more than the paltry two weeks recommended by the CDC, a far too optimistic guideline that fails to provide sufficient safety.

You also want to ensure you protect your mental safety. That means replacing the kind of entertainment and exercise you used to do outside and/or with other people by indoor solitary activities, in case of extreme lockdowns or self-quarantine due to COVID-19 in your household. Figure out a way to keep yourself physically healthy through indoor exercises, ranging from yoga to weight lifting. Take up new hobbies, ranging from crafting to do-it-yourself home improvement. Develop new ways of entertaining yourself, from virtual reality to board games with members of your household. Take up gratitude journaling and other tools to improve your mood and advance personal growth. Limit your exposure to anxiety and sadness-inducing news stories and consider teletherapy as needed.

An important part of protecting your mental and physical safety alike involves getting the right information, in the context of widespread information about COVID-19, including unfortunately by some prominent political and civic leaders. In a book I co-wrote with Tim Ward, called *Pro Truth: A Practical Plan for Putting Truth Back into Politics*, I describe how to figure out what is true in the firehose of information flowing through our media channels. A good shortcut to do so involves relying on information coming from public figures that signed the Pro-Truth Pledge (at ProTruthPledge.org), which involves following 12 simple truth-oriented behaviors.

- *Verify:* fact-check information to confirm it is true before accepting and sharing it
- *Balance:* share the whole truth, even if some aspects do not support my opinion
- *Cite:* share my sources so that others can verify my information
- *Clarify:* distinguish between my opinion and the facts
- *Acknowledge:* acknowledge when others share true information, even when we disagree otherwise
- *Reevaluate:* reevaluate if my information is challenged, retract it if I cannot verify it
- *Defend:* defend others when they come under attack

for sharing true information, even when we disagree otherwise

- *Align:* align my opinions and my actions with true information
- *Fix:* ask people to retract information that reliable sources have disproved even if they are my allies
- *Educate:* compassionately inform those around me to stop using unreliable sources even if these sources support my opinion
- *Defer:* recognize the opinions of experts as more likely to be accurate when the facts are disputed
- *Celebrate:* celebrate those who retract incorrect statements and update their beliefs toward the truth

Any public figure or private citizen, including yourself, can go to that website and sign the pledge to show their commitment to these values, which helps create a more truthful world, and to encourage others to sign it as well. You can also see who else signed it – including public figures such as politicians and media professionals – and pay attention to these people, while making sure to hold them accountable per the pledge accountability mechanism.

Connection

Protecting your mental safety brings us to the second fundamental need: connection to others. It's a topic I describe in much more depth in my best-seller, *The Blindspots Between Us: How to Overcome Unconscious Cognitive Bias and Build Better Relationships*.

First, consider your immediate connections with members of the household.

If you have a romantic partner in your household, you'll have to figure out how to interact in a healthy manner given that you're together 24/7. You'll likely get into each other's spaces and on each other's nerves. It's much wiser to anticipate and work out these problems in advance than have them blow up down the road.

The same principle applies to other members of your family. If you have older children who moved home after university closed, or younger children who aren't going to school after it closed, you'll need to figure out how to deal with them being cooped up inside.

You'll have to put more thought into dealing with older adults over 60 or anyone with underlying health conditions in your household (including yourself if you fit either category). Given their much greater vulnerability to COVID-19, you and other members of your household need to take serious measures to prevent them from getting ill. That means being more careful yourself than you would otherwise be, since over half of all those with COVID-19 have no or light symptoms. Remember: don't kill Grandma. And don't let other members of your household kill Grandma.

Second, what about your connection to those who you care about who aren't part of your household?

Your romantic partner might not be part of your household. Depending on how vulnerable to COVID-19 you and other members of your household might be, you might choose to take the risk of physical intimacy with your romantic partner, but you have to make this decision consciously rather than casually. Or you might choose to have a socially-distant relationship, meeting at a distance of 10 feet or by videoconference.

The same goes for your friends. You can't have a beer with them or meet for lunch in person, at least closer than 10 feet. You'll need to figure out effective ways of interacting with them virtually during this difficult time of the next several years.

What about your family members who aren't in your household? You'll need to develop virtual interactions with them as well. Older family members or those with underlying health conditions are a particular concern. If you're one of the many people in their 30s, 40s, or 50s supporting an older family member who is living independently but requires occasional help, you're going to face particular challenges with protecting them from the possibility of you infecting them with COVID-19. Even if they don't require in-person help from you, many will have difficulty adapting to virtual interaction and will struggle to cope.

It may prove especially difficult if they get sick. I personally really struggled when my dad, who is 79 and lives in the COVID-19 hotspot of New York City, got sick with what was very likely COVID-19 in early April. I live in Columbus, Ohio, and in a different situation, would have hopped on a plane to help my mom take care of him. But of course, doing so wasn't feasible in the middle of the early stages of the pandemic. I was left to wonder and worry as he suffered with worsening flu-like symptoms, including the difficulty breathing that is particularly associated with COVID-19. He recovered eventually, very fortunately, but it's something that you need to be prepared to deal with for older relatives in your life.

You'll also want to think about how you'll revise your community activities: faith-based groups, clubs, nonprofit activism, and so on. For instance, you should definitely avoid church services for now, but fortunately many churches offer video worship services, and that will have to do. You can take the lead in your club on moving to videoconference meetings. You will have to figure out how to replace your in-person volunteering, perhaps with virtual volunteering or with donations.

Self-esteem

Finally, address the third fundamental need of self-esteem, which refers to your self-confidence, self-respect, and sense of mastery over your fate. Thinking through and making a plan for addressing your physiological and mental safety and your relationships during the next several years of the pandemic will help you strengthen your sense of control and confidence. You'll also want to think about other areas that you can further master in this time of restrictions and limitations.

Your career offers one obvious area. If you're not currently in a job that allows work from home, and aren't working in a critically important area for addressing the pandemic such as healthcare, start investing in a career transition to one that permits virtual service delivery. The same applies if you're working in a role or industry severely impacted by the pandemic, such as in-person entertainment, restaurants, airlines, and so on.

For example, I make much of my money from public speaking and training. All my events were cancelled due to the pandemic. As a result, I quickly transitioned to virtual presentations. Some of my coaching clients had to make more major shifts, not simply changing their service delivery model but switching from one industry to another.

Another area is taking up home-based productive activities that help make your life better during the pandemic, such as home improvements, indoor or outdoor gardening, cooking, and so on. Doing so is empowering and helps you develop your sense of mastery over your environment.

You can also work on mastering new skills or further developing existing ones. Being at home offers a great opportunity to learn an instrument, pick up coding skills, or try to make a viral YouTube video.

Exploration

Such mastery feeds into the higher-level self-actualization needs, specifically the need for exploration. That need refers to a desire to learn and understand the world. Exploration in this sense is driven not by fear and anxiety – such as the watching of daily news briefings on the pandemic – but by the thrill of discovery and curiosity about the novel, the challenging, the unknown. Exploration requires going outside your comfort zone and experiencing the growth associated with doing so.

While you're restricted by being at home, you have a universe of information available for exploration through the Internet. Decide on an area of discovery that you will pursue, something genuinely challenging.

You might take this time for an exploration of a different culture. Take the time to learn about, say, the daily life of people in the Philippines, and connect with some of them on Facebook to have conversations about their experiences and beliefs. Having done so myself, I can attest it's a difficult experience of personal growth to grasp how similar they are to me, yet how different at the same time.

Perhaps you can take some time to explore volunteering virtually for a good cause, experiencing personal growth in doing so. For instance, during this pandemic many people – especially older adults – experience even more social isolation than they did before. A number of nonprofits provide an opportunity for you to connect with them through phone calls and video chats, giving them a sense of companionship.

Love

That latter form of exploration also contributes to the second aspect of self-actualization highlighted by Kaufman: expressing love toward others, by which he means making a positive impact on their lives. By volunteering virtually to provide companionship to lonely elder adult strangers, you satisfy your need to make that positive impact.

Of course, you can also bring that love toward your existing relationships. Besides simply maintaining your connections – a fundamental need – you can also, without any expectations in return, devote your energy toward improving the lives of those with whom you have relationships. Perhaps you can lead the way in organizing virtual parties or game nights. Maybe you can send some healthy fruit to a friend's house, just because. Surprise your romantic partner with an unexpected date night.

Purpose

The other critical aspect of self-actualization involves developing, refining, and pursuing your sense of meaning and purpose, a topic I explore in much more depth in my *Find Your Purpose Using Science*. In the context of the pandemic, it's even more important to seek proactively a sense that you are contributing to something you're passionate about that's bigger than yourself, a personal mission of service that offers you fulfillment and contentment.

Some might find their sense of purpose in raising their kids and otherwise taking care of their friends and family, and that's fine. You might focus on improving your local community, such as encouraging others to stay at home during the pandemic through blogging about your fun at-home adventures, and that's fine as well. Others (including myself) may emphasize serving their society through spreading valuable messages about how to adapt to and survive and thrive during the pandemic. Or maybe you might continue addressing issues you focused on before the pandemic, for instance accountants who volunteered to do taxes for low-income people continuing to do so, except via virtual means. Whatever you do, evaluate how much it contributes to your sense of purpose, and revise your activities to help further develop that sense within yourself.

Of course, it's not only individuals who need to adapt their households and careers; companies and other organizations need to adapt as well, and that's what the next chapter is about. In the meantime, check out more resources based on the book, such as a workbook, recorded webinar, and the most current research-based findings on how to adapt and plan most effectively for COVID-19, at https://disasteravoidanceexperts.com/adapt.

Chapter 3

How to Adapt to the New Abnormal of COVID-19: Companies and Other Organizations

As the pandemic broke out, companies and other organizations overwhelmingly turned to their existing emergency business continuity plan and then simply continued with that plan as the pandemic continued. Yet continuing with emergency measures throughout the minimal two years of the pandemic is not wise, to say the least. A business continuity plan is meant for a week or two, a month at most if it's a really good plan, before things start returning to normal (I tell you this as someone who helped businesses and nonprofits design many business continuity plans).

Unfortunately, we will not return to the "normal" status quo ante pandemic. Ever.

Do you think that, even in the most optimistic scenario of only two years of waves of stricter and looser shutdowns and social distancing, our society will ever be the same? Of course not. And let's remember that we shouldn't plan for the most optimistic scenario, so assume a five-year horizon instead of two years.

While we'll cover that longer-term time horizon in the next chapters, in the meantime you need to adapt to the next few months, not the next few years. And your emergency measures won't cut it.

You need to accept the current reality of ongoing waves of restrictions as the new abnormal, instead of a temporary emergency. That means fundamentally changing your business model if you want your company, nonprofit, or other organization to survive and thrive during these troubled years.

Internal Business Model

First, look at your internal systems, processes, and internal organization. While the vast majority of companies and other organizations have already switched to virtual work to some extent, you have to make virtual work the default for the next several years for as many employees as physically possible (yes, including sales, fundraising, and other positions where in-person contact seems critically important for relationship building). Even during looser periods, avoid in-person staff meetings: about half of all those infected with COVID-19 don't have any significant symptoms and don't know they're sick, and many companies had COVID-19 sweep through employee ranks due to such meetings.

I strongly suggest my clients sell or end the lease on their office space, whenever this is possible. Doing so burns your bridges and marks a point of no return for you; it also helps you improve your cash position during this difficult time without incurring the kind of reputational penalties or cutting off access to government subsidies associated with laying off staff.

Having made the switch, you have to address the specific challenges associated with shifting from in-office to virtual teams. It's useful to learn here from the example of organizations that had mostly or completely virtual teams already, such as Basecamp, Upworthy, or this book's publisher, John Hunt Publishing.

Immediately after the rapid onset of the pandemic, everyone fell into emergency mode, which prevented a lot of problems typically associated with this change. However, your staff can only function in emergency mode for so long, before coming to realize they're in a new abnormal, and adjusting to the long haul. You'll have to deal with several important issues:

1. Motivation and engagement
2. Effective communication

3. Noticing and solving problems and conflicts
4. Cultivating trust
5. Security
6. Accountability

Motivation and Engagement

Already before the pandemic, US workplaces experienced serious challenges in employee engagement and motivation. The 2018 Gallup Engagement Survey found only 34% of the employees felt truly "engaged," meaning enthusiastic about and committed to their work, ready to take initiative and make sacrifices if needed for the sake of their company. Most – 53% – belonged to the "not engaged" category, those who do the minimum required to keep their job and ready to leave for a slightly better position. The rest, 13%, were "actively disengaged," actively looking for a new position and undermining their company.

In the early days and weeks of the pandemic-induced shift to working from home, the adrenaline rush of the fight-or-flight response boosted motivation and engagement. Of course, such boosts fade pretty quickly. Now, you need to figure out how to keep your staff motivated and engaged in the context of working from home.

Doing so provides a series of challenges. In a gradual and voluntary switch to working from home, an employee has plenty of time to set up a home office that minimizes distractions and maximizes productivity. They're also highly motivated to demonstrate to often-skeptical supervisors that the shift will not decrease productivity and indeed increase it. The switch is usually gradual, with an employee working from home part of the time, enabling any problems to be worked out, including with motivation. Furthermore, employees who switch to working from home are often self-motivated, not requiring the presence of others to inspire them; they're also usually introverted, drawing energy from being alone rather than from other people.

None of this applies to the abrupt shift of all non-essential personnel to working from home. The psychological makeup of many of your employees makes it hard for them to be productive without other people around. They're either not self-motivated, extroverted, or both. You need to figure out how to effectively motivate such people, which used to happen naturally in the office environment.

You also have to figure out how to help them set up a workspace at home free from distractions. Remember, they might very well have to deal with a house full of unruly children, or adults acting like children in the context of the disruption caused by the pandemic. They might also be figuring out how to be a caretaker for older adults while avoiding infecting them. Of course, the other challenging conditions of the pandemic might be undercutting their motivations, ranging from the need to secure consumables to maintain their mental well-being to protecting their relationships, as the previous section described.

While some will be able to figure all this out on their own, many will not, especially in the context of the overwhelm, anxiety, and depression induced by COVID-19. It's the organization's responsibility to support them and provide them with resources, guidance, and training that will help them do so and keep them productive, motivated, and engaged with their work.

Effective Communication

Next, you'll need to ensure effective communication in your virtual team. It's notoriously hard to communicate effectively, due in part to cognitive biases that impede our communication. For example, the illusion of transparency causes us to believe that our mental state – thoughts and feelings – are much more transparent than they actually are. Thus, we assume that others understand the messages we're trying to send, while in reality they miss a large percentage of what we're trying to convey.

The illusion of transparency is just one of many reasons

why many experts made a good living before the pandemic helping leaders and teams improve their communication (full disclosure: that's one of the areas where I often help clients). Effective communication becomes much more difficult when in-office teams become virtual teams, in my experience helping individuals and organizations make this transition.

One of the biggest problems stems from much more communication shifting to text – e-mail, text messages, or messages in collaboration apps such as Slack, Trello, or Asana. As a result, much of the nonverbal communication is lost, leading to a huge increase in miscommunication. You might have heard that only 7% of all communication is verbal and 93% is nonverbal. That statistic is false: it's based on a limited and poorly-designed experiment where prospects study salespeople and assess how much credibility to assign to words vs. body language and tone.

Still, you do lose some important aspects of communication by losing nonverbals. First, you're losing most of your ability to read the emotions underlying the words. Given that how we feel motivates much of how we behave and what we think, this represents an enormous loss in understanding what the person actually means to convey.

Envision observing a meeting of the leadership team of a middle-market company, where the company's Chief Operating Officer says, with a confident posture and a cheery voice, "I think Mike should lead this product launch." You'd probably think that she is confident about the product and Mike's leadership. Now, imagine the COO saying the same words, except crossing her arms in a defensive posture, and using a dismissive tone. You'd likely guess that she has little confidence in Mike or the success of the launch. The body language and tone completely change the meaning associated with the words, yet text-based communication fails to convey this underlying meaning.

Similarly, you lose the ability to observe the nonverbal

response to the communication. Let's say the COO makes her statement with a confident posture and cheery voice, and you observe Mike leaning forward, smiling, and nodding his head. You'd probably assume Mike is enthusiastic about the project and excited to lead the launch. Now imagine the COO says the same thing, and you see Mike pushing his chair back, crossing his arms in a defensive position, and shaking his head from side to side. It's a good bet that, for some reason, Mike doesn't want to be stuck with the role of launch leader. Over text, there's no way of observing Mike's response.

Now imagine these sorts of text-based communications multiplied by the daily interactions between team members, and it becomes clear why misunderstandings drastically increase in shifting to virtual teams.

Phone calls and videoconferences help address these problems to some extent. Still, even videoconferencing doesn't convey nearly as much body language as in-person meetings. When you have eight people in small boxes on your laptop screen – or even worse, your phone – it's hard to read their body language well. Also, you only get the body language of facial expressions, and miss the 90% of the body that's not on camera.

Videoconferences can be especially problematic for older employees, often the ones in leadership positions, who feel uncomfortable with the newfangled technology, or are hard-of-hearing. On the one hand, they might inadvertently make a whole range of mistakes when using videoconference software. On the other, they don't react naturally on camera, resulting in more difficulty reading the underlying emotions behind their body language.

It's vital to train and coach employees on how to communicate effectively in virtual team settings. You can read more about doing so in another book in the Resilience Series from John Hunt Publishing, *Virtually Speaking – Communicating at a Distance*, by Teresa Erickson and Tim Ward.

Yet the vast majority of companies and other organizations, in the context of the pandemic, are ignoring this critically important professional development need. They will reap what they sow, as the seeds of miscommunication planted now will grow into choking weeds that strangle effective teamwork in the next few months and years of the pandemic.

Noticing and Solving Problems and Conflicts

A related area, one that requires just as much investment in professional development, is the ability to notice and solve problems and conflicts.

In the office, face-to-face interactions help employees notice problems and nip them in the bud. You pop into each other's office or run into each other in the hallway or share a meal in the cafeteria, talk briefly about the project you're working on together, and catch potential problems while getting on the same page about next steps. Sometimes, you solve the problem immediately. At other times, you have to spend some time by yourself or together collaborating to solve the problem. Occasionally, you have to bring the problem to your supervisors or the rest of the team, getting their input on solving it.

Easy, right? Happens all the time naturally, as a result of close proximity of people working on the same initiatives.

Well, it won't happen in virtual settings. There's no natural way to have these casual interactions that are surprisingly vital to effective collaboration and teamwork. Over the next few weeks and months, you'll start to notice more and more problems coming up, the kinds of things that were easily noticed and addressed in the past, throwing multiple wrenches into the machinery of your organization. To address this challenge, you need to provide training to your staff in noticing and solving problems in virtual settings effectively.

Pay particular attention to people-related problems, otherwise known as conflicts. Body language and voice tone are especially important to noticing brewing conflicts, and your staff will have much less signals of these people problems going forward. So you'll want to provide specific training in noticing and addressing conflicts in virtual teams.

Also consider how to address people problems related to the intra-office grapevine. No, it hasn't disappeared when you moved into a virtual team setting. It's just taken a different form: text messages, private phone and videoconference calls, and so on. Figure out how to tap into and manage the grapevine in order to gauge employee morale and to notice and head off brewing conflicts.

Cultivating Trust and Building Relationships

Another area to address, vital for effective communication and addressing problems alike, is cultivating trust and building relationships within your team. Don't underestimate this one!

In office settings, it's easy to build relationships and trust. You meet by the watercooler or over lunch in the breakroom and chat about what you did this weekend, your passion for the local sports ball team, the latest accomplishments by your kids, your vacation plans, your hobbies, the latest dumb thing a local politician said, and so on. Such social grooming activities offer a critically important opportunity for people to get to know each other as human beings, developing relationships and learning to trust one another.

There's a reason teams that start off virtual but later meet in person at a company event together perform much better after doing so: they have a sense of each other as human beings, not simply names on e-mails or tiny faces in videoconference windows. Such face-to-face meetings lead to much more collaborative relationships, better communication, and decreased conflicts. By contrast, teams that shift from in-person settings to virtual ones gradually lose that sense of shared humanity, leading to more tensions and stress.

To guard against that requires a proactive replacement of relationship cultivation and trust building. It's not about training, it's about policies.

For instance, for one consulting client, a financial services company of 130 people that made the transition to a virtual team several years before the pandemic hit, I helped establish a virtual watercooler. They used Slack as their collaboration software and established a "Morning Updates" channel there. Every morning, all employees send a message answering the following questions:

1. How are you doing overall?
2. How are you feeling right now?
3. What's been interesting in your life recently outside of work?
4. What's going on in your work: what's going well, and what are some challenges?
5. What is one thing about you that most other team members do not know about?

Employees are encouraged to post photos or videos as part of their answers. They are also asked to respond to at least three other employees who made an update that day.

Note that most of these questions are about life outside of work, and aim to help people get to know each other. They humanize virtual team members to each other, helping them get to know each other as human beings, or keeping that connection if they had already known each other from in-office collaboration.

There's also one work question, focusing on helping team members learn what others are working on right now. That question helps them collaborate together more effectively.

In addition, there's another channel within the company's Slack that's called "Life Stuff." There, anyone who feels inspired can share about what's going in their life and respond to others who do so. The combination of mandated morning updates combined with the autonomy of the "Life Stuff" channel provides a good balance for building relationships and cultivating trust that fits the different preferences and personalities of the company's employees.

This tactic is one among many that you can use to bring about the strategic outcome of maintaining trust through building relationships. Consider what would work best for your virtual team. Another book in the Resilience Series from John Hunt Publishing covers this topic in much more depth, *Virtual Teams: Holding the Center When You Can't Meet Face-to-Face* by Carlos Valdes-Dapena.

Security

Now that so many people are working at home, you have much more security-related exposure that you need to address. Cybersecurity is one big area. Cybercrime of all sorts has increased significantly with the pandemic: ransomware, malicious domains, phishing and spear phishing, and so on. Criminals know that huge numbers of employees are working from home, where their computer setup is, on average, much less secure than the office. Moreover, in their home employees aren't used to following the kind of security protocols they follow at the office. Finally, the pandemic itself gives more opportunities to criminals, who are, for example, sending phishing e-mails designed to look like communications from the CDC.

Another is physical security. With the recession accompanying the pandemic, crime is likely to increase. The breakdown of social bonds will also likely contribute to crime.

You need to help your employees improve their cybersecurity and physical security alike. Create protocols and policies, and pay for services and products, to help your employees be more secure.

Accountability

In-office environments allow for natural ways to hold employees accountable. Leaders can easily walk around the office, visually observing what's going on and checking in with their direct reports on their projects. Observing interactions around the office and people's body language helps them read whether employees are on top of their work or if they need support and encouragement to improve their performance. In turn, the sight of supervisors walking around reminds team members to focus on their tasks.

So do the daily interactions with their colleagues in the office, where team members passing each other in the hallway or popping into each other's office can ask, "John, when do you think you'll get me that marketing brochure draft," holding each other accountable. It's much easier to ignore an e-mail with that question than someone stopping you in the hallway or standing in the doorway to your office.

You'll need to replace that accountability with a different structure. It should enable accountability up the chain of command and peer-to-peer accountability for people at the same level, within teams and across teams to those in different business units.

For instance, for the financial services company mentioned above, we established a weekly report system. Each employee would submit a publicly-visible report in a Slack channel about what they did that week, highlighting tasks where they collaborated with other people and using the tagging function to notify those people about their report submission. Those others would then need either to confirm that the employee indeed did the task to the standards required, or provide constructive critical feedback on the performance of the task. That system enabled both hierarchical and peer-to-peer accountability, and you should consider what tactic you'll use to accomplish the same outcome.

External Business Model

While the way companies and other organizations fundamentally transform their internal business model to adapt to the pandemic is broadly similar, the external business model will be more varied. It depends on what kind of product or service you're providing, and whether you're a for-profit company or one of several types of nonprofit organizations: charities, associations, municipalities, etc.

What will be similar in all cases will be the need to figure out how to:

1. Deliver offerings virtually
2. Cultivate relationships virtually
3. Manage external stakeholder disruptions
4. Anticipate socioeconomic shifts
5. Prepare for unknown unknowns
6. Outcompete your competition

Delivering Offerings Virtually

Your ability to provide your products or services in virtual or at least socially distanced contexts will depend, of course, on the nature of what you're providing. For some, it will be easy: instead of going through retail channels, you'll just shift to direct-to-consumer offerings and/or online marketplaces.

For others, it will prove more of a challenge. The company I run, the boutique consulting, coaching, and training firm Disaster Avoidance Experts, provided most of its services through in-person engagements. Fortunately, we also had some virtual service offerings – classes, webinars, and coaching – and are now focusing on providing only these (which includes convincing some clients that the events they think they'll be able to run because "this will all blow over quickly" will not happen).

Other professional services providers will also struggle to provide their services virtually, ranging from doctors to lawyers to accountants to bankers. Depending on your industry, you'll have to deal with problems ranging from regulations to client pushback. Indeed, a company of just over a hundred lawyers that I'm helping transition to a virtual business model is finding the latter to be the most difficult issue.

Many clients, especially older ones, want to get legal advice face-to-face, especially on more touchy subjects. In other cases, the lawyers are finding that they're having much more trouble convincing their clients to do the right thing compared to when they could engage in face-to-face interactions. To address this issue, we're focusing on having lawyers convey to their clients that this pandemic will not blow over quickly and that the clients will face major legal liabilities and in general a lot of problems if they don't adapt to virtual interactions and social distancing. You need to make the same case explicitly to your clients.

In some cases, even personal care service providers have found ways to provide their expertise virtually. For example, some savvy hair stylists are providing their customers with coaching on maintaining their haircuts, sending coloring kits customized to each client's needs, and setting up YouTube channels, podcasts, and blogs to maintain their revenue. Still, I'd advise the large majority of restaurants, in-person entertainment venues, and so on to consider how they can make a major pivot to a different industry, as the next five years will not be good ones for them.

Cultivate Relationships Virtually

It's just as important to cultivate existing relationships with your external stakeholders – clients, suppliers, service providers, investors, civic and political leaders, and others – as it is to maintain relationships among your staff. You'll also need to build new relationships with external stakeholders, ranging from prospects for your offerings to new suppliers, service providers and so on that you need to survive and thrive in the context of the shifts associated with the pandemic.

Doing both is much harder via virtual means. You'll have to figure out how to cultivate trust, communicate effectively, and notice and resolve problems and conflicts, just as you do with team members. Such stakeholder engagement in virtual settings requires making a clear plan for this area and serious investment into professional development training, especially for salespeople and client management staff in companies and fundraisers in nonprofits. Keep in mind the silver lining that, by establishing new relationships via virtual means, you have a global market of potential clients, investors, and other external stakeholders.

Manage External Stakeholder Disruptions

Many of your stakeholders will face a range of disruptions in their activities. Plenty will not be as savvy as you, failing to plan for the long-term disruption associated with the pandemic even in the most optimistic scenario. They'll instead rely on their emergency plans and government stimulus to carry them through what they wrongly perceive as a brief period of disruption until things go back to normal.

While you can try to help them see the error of their ways, in many cases you will be unable to get them to take off their rose-colored glasses. In those cases, you'll have to protect yourself against them falling into normalcy bias and planning fallacy.

A case in point from one of my clients, a Midwestern manufacturing company of several hundred people that produces a wide range of heavy equipment. It relies on six major suppliers for component parts, and four of these suppliers had their head stuck in the proverbial sand about the reality of the long-term impact of the pandemic. While my client's leadership managed to convince one to take the long-term impact seriously, the other three refused to do so. Thus, my client is right now working on contingency plans for shifting their supply chains to more reliable partners.

In other cases, you will have to decide how long to wait for business partners who are willing to acknowledge the situation, yet are struggling due to the impact of the pandemic. One of my consulting clients, an Electronic Health Record company of several hundred people, has been having trouble with collecting accounts receivable from their healthcare clients. Still, given the cash crunch experienced by hospitals hit hard by the pandemic, the client decided to give them a break and permit much more generous repayment terms.

Anticipate Socioeconomic Shifts

Guess what? After two, five, or even more years of constant restrictions and loosenings, of social distance and virtual interactions, people will have different wants, desires, expectations, norms, and habits, both in their personal and professional life. The better you can anticipate and get ahead of these shifts, the better off you will be positioned to not simply survive, but also thrive in the new abnormal.

What matters most for you will be determined by your industry, naturally. Retail will not come back nearly as strong even after stores reopen, with COVID-19 exacerbating the shift toward online shopping. In entertainment, virtual and augmented reality will take off, as opposed to puttering along as it has for the last few years, despite all the predictions made by futurists. You'll see more widespread adoption of robotics in areas like home care and self-driving cars. Analyze what's going on in your industry wisely, keeping in mind that you're likely going to underestimate the changes intuitively due to anchoring.

Prepare for Unknown Unknowns

In a press briefing on February 12, 2002, Donald Rumsfeld, at the time US Secretary of Defense, said, "there are also unknown unknowns – the ones we don't know we don't know. And if one looks throughout the history of our country and other free countries, it is the latter category that tend to be the difficult ones." In his 2007 book *The Black Swan: The Impact of the Highly Improbable*, Nassim Nicholas Taleb describes a specific type of unknown unknown as "black swans": surprising, low-likelihood, and high-impact events. He convincingly argues that we don't prepare nearly as much as we should for black swans; given what we know about normalcy bias, the reason for that stems from the deep workings of the human brain.

Fortunately, awareness of this vulnerability helps lead to its cure. Taleb highlights how we can scan the future and reflect on possible unknown unknowns, thus turning such events from "black swans" to "grey swans" by removing the "surprise" aspect of black swans. As an example, it's certainly possible to envision a successful major cyberattack on the US that takes out the power grid for most of Ohio, Michigan, and Pennsylvania during the November 3 election. Cyberattackers have been testing US defenses periodically, for example in a March 5, 2019 attack, and it's quite possible that they know enough to launch a successful attack at the worst possible time. Imagine the kind of chaos it would cause politically to have the election disrupted in these three key swing states that will likely determine the Presidency, Senate, and House composition, added on top of the very likely growing second outbreak of the COVID-19 pandemic.

By envisioning this scenario, we've now turned it into a grey swan – a low-likelihood, high-impact event – instead of a black swan, by removing the "surprise." So if your organization happens to be located in a swing state, you will hopefully be on the lookout for such disruptions around the election. In the context of the major disruption caused by the pandemic, you need to be especially prepared for other disruptors that can damage you or your external stakeholders.

You can envision and prepare for a whole range of scenarios relevant to your industry. Say you're working a lot with

Australian collaborators. Having seen the impact of wildfires there this year in December and January, and likely felt their impact on your business, you would not be wise if you didn't prepare for the possibility of the same next year.

Some things you can't foresee: these represent true black swans. Some come from nature, such as a major asteroid strike that takes out your main factory. Some come from other people, such as a hostile activist investor taking a stake in your company and trying to take over the Board of Directors.

To deal with such true black swans, you need to invest strategically into reserving a sufficient cushion of cash, making effective backup plans, and building up social capital. It might feel uncomfortable and put you under pressure to hold excess cash, but don't give in to the temptation to "put it to use" by investing into projects or buying back stocks: a good rule of thumb is to hold back enough to weather a yearlong loss of revenue. Cash combined with a backup plan for your production needs would help you address an asteroid strike, fire, or other disaster in your factory, especially if the insurance company drags its feet or tries to invoke the "act of God" clause on the meteor. Cash combined with social capital, namely very positive relations with your major investors, can help you beat back a hostile activist investor. And of course, cash and strategic planning can help you address all sorts of grey swans.

Outcompete Your Competition

By taking all of these steps early, you will have a major competitive advantage. The large majority of your competitors will be falling for the planning fallacy, the normalcy bias, and other oh-so-tempting dangerous judgment errors. As a result, they'll waste their time, money, and other resources on unrealistic plans, dreams, and hopes.

That's the time to make your move. Right now, you should work on how to adapt your organization to the pandemic and make a clear long-term plan preparing for a realistic and even pessimistic scenario. Then, at the right time, be ready to use the consequences of your competitive advantage to seize market share from your competitors who are inadequately prepared for the reality of COVID-19.

Research their clients, and decide who will be your first targets, based on which ones of your competitors you think will start failing first. Approach them early offering to be a backup just in case things go south with your competitor. Some will want to start a conversation. Others will at least keep you in mind for the future.

Besides market share, prepare to seize the resources of your competitors. Some will be hobbled, while others go bankrupt. Be ready to hire highly-qualified employees who will be let go by those companies. Anticipate buying the material resources of organizations undergoing a fire sale.

You'll need a combination of cash and strategic planning to enable you to do so effectively. And it's long-term strategic planning in the context of uncertainty to which we'll turn in the next chapter. Also, make sure to get more resources relevant to the book, including a workbook, recorded webinar, and the most recent evidence on how to adapt and plan most effectively for COVID-19, at https://disasteravoidanceexperts.com/adapt.

Chapter 4

How to Make a Strategic Plan for the New Abnormal of COVID-19 and the Post-Pandemic Society

Did you know that the typical five-year strategic planning forecasts perform about as well as dart-throwing chimpanzees? Studies show that even the most skilled forecasters among us perform no better than chance on economic predictions five years out, as described in Philip Tetlock's excellent *Superforecasting: The Art and Science of Prediction*.

Once again, cognitive biases are to blame, both the ones we discussed earlier and some other ones of particular relevance to planning and predictions. For example, the *overconfidence bias* describes our excessive confidence about our decisions: we tend to decide too quickly, without evaluating sufficient alternative options and future possibility. Scholars have found that business leaders at all levels make bad decisions due to overconfidence, especially those who have been most successful in the past. They tend to believe themselves infallible, a cognitive bias called the *bias blind spot*. To quote Proverbs 16:18, "Pride goeth before destruction, and an haughty spirit before a fall."

Another mental blindspot of relevance to predictions and plans, the *optimism bias*, causes us to be too optimistic about the future. The optimism bias is my biggest weakness, as I intuitively emphasize opportunities and feel hopeful about what will occur while disregarding risks and ignoring threats; my gut reaction is to see the grass as green on the other side of the hill, even though it's too often yellow.

One that harms badly our predictions and plans, the *confirmation bias*, refers to our tendency to look for information that confirms our beliefs, and ignore information that does not. Thus, those who have hold to a clear ideological lens and strong opinions about how the world should work make worse predictions than those who can put aside their initial perspectives and focus on accuracy above all. Yet even then, accuracy above chance when predicting more than a year out is hard to achieve.

Tragically, even popular strategic business analyses meant to address the weaknesses of human predictions on strategic planning are deeply flawed. They give a false sense of comfort and security to those who use them, leading you into the exact disasters that you seek to avoid.

Take the most popular of them, the SWOT analysis, where you try to figure out the Strengths, Weaknesses, Opportunities, and Threats facing you. SWOT doesn't account for cognitive biases, which twist the results in predictable and systematic ways. When taking on new coaching and consulting clients, I always ask whether they did a SWOT. In literally all cases when they did one, I've seen their cognitive biases – confirmation bias, overconfidence bias, and others – lead them to disregard risks, minimize weaknesses, overestimate rewards, and inflate strengths.

With all this in mind you should not make a typical strategic plan to address COVID-19 and prepare for the post-pandemic society, especially given the challenges posed by normalcy bias, hyperbolic discounting, planning fallacy, and other cognitive biases discussed that harm our decision-making around the pandemic in particular. Instead, you should use the "Defend Your Future" technique, an approach I developed informed by cognitive neuroscience and behavioral economics, combined with extensive experience helping clients prepare for uncertain futures.

"Defend Your Future" enables you to scan the future and plan for a variety of possible scenarios. You'll anticipate and solve problems associated with each potential scenario, as well as identify and figure out how to seize opportunities in each scenario. You'll also reserve and invest resources according to your needs in each scenario. That way, no matter what future comes about, you will be prepared to meet it effectively and successfully.

Defend Your Future: Potential Scenarios

Your specific approach to planning should depend on whether you are doing so as a household or as an organization, and how many different people are involved in creating your plans. At the minimum, you should plan for at least three possible future scenarios.

First, plan for an optimistic future. At the very simplest and most basic level, that might involve two factors. First, the government in your region handles the management of the waves of restrictions and loosenings to address COVID-19 outbreaks very competently in balancing health and economic concerns. Second, by the beginning of 2022, over half of the population in your region – all frontline workers and anyone in the more vulnerable groups over 60 and with underlying health conditions – have been vaccinated with an effective vaccine, meaning one that prevents over 95% of infections.

How much do you trust your national and regional officials to show excellent competence? I'd say fewer than 1 in 10 deserve an "A" for their handling of the pandemic's initial stages, and this trend, I suspect, will continue for their handling of the pandemic going forward.

How much faith should you put in the first wave of vaccines? Recall that most vaccines don't make it through the testing process even during the best of times. How much more would that apply to vaccines rushed through development and into testing with minimal safeguards for failure?

Given that, I'd say the probability for this optimistic scenario is under 5%. That might sound shockingly low to you, at least if you're reading this book in the Summer of 2020 and keep hearing that various vaccines are being developed. Yet I want to remind you it takes over a year to test vaccines and then over half a year to produce enough for mass use. So I strongly suggest you check yourself for the normalcy bias and other cognitive biases that make you underestimate the length of time to dealing with the pandemic.

Next, plan for a moderate scenario. For example, say the government in your region does a moderately competent job, resulting in 10% less economic activity and 10% more deaths than would be the case with the most effective balance. Also, an effective vaccine is not found and made widely available until early 2024.

This scenario is much more likely, because many national and regional governments have not performed well in addressing the initial stages of COVID-19 and I don't believe they will suddenly and magically get the management of restrictions and loosenings right. Neither do I trust the hype of a number of medical companies rushing through the early stages of the vaccine development process, as they're much more likely to make mistakes that will prevent their vaccine from making it through the trials.

I'd give this scenario a ballpark of 70% likelihood. To be more specific, if I had to bet, at the time of book publication I'd gladly take a bet saying that a vaccine will be widely available in the US and UK between late 2022 and late 2026. Early 2024 serves as a convenient median for developing your plan.

Now step back and feel how weird, uncomfortable, and distressing it feels to envision planning for 2024. Try to get over that gut intuition and internalize the idea that it's about simple math, combined with realistic estimates of competence of government officials, medical companies, and regulators. It may feel unreal, but you will do yourself no favors by relying on hope as a strategy.

Finally, prepare for a pessimistic scenario. Say the government in your region does a bad job, resulting in 25% less economic activity and 25% more deaths than would be the case with the most effective balance. Also, a vaccine is not found and made widely available until early 2027.

A number of government officials have behaved surprisingly incompetently, failing their citizens badly. Unfortunately, both the US and UK national governments fall into this category. By acting atrociously slowly when instituting shutdowns, they let the initial outbreaks grow much worse than they needed to be in their countries.

The result? A much higher death toll and a greatly increased economic cost. The latter comes both from the economic consequences of many people dying and the much more extensive eventual shutdowns and social distancing required to control the major outbreaks in each country.

While the UK's approach is much more centralized, in the US the state governors have final say on the COVID-19 response in their states. Some have acted quickly to shut down non-essential services and enforce social distancing, minimizing the death toll, such as the Republican Governor of Ohio Mike DeWine. Others have not, such as the Republican Governor of Florida Ron DeSantis, resulting in a spike of deaths. You may get unlucky with your national and/or regional government's poor response.

The whole world may get unlucky with vaccines. On the one hand, the novel coronavirus that causes COVID-19 fortunately mutates more slowly than the flu: good news for the potential of an effective vaccine. On the other hand, we have a number of reports at the time of the book's publication of some people who contracted COVID-19 and then recovered but got sick again. While scientists are studying what happened, such news does not bode well for an effective vaccine in the medium term.

Given this evidence, I'd say there's a 25% chance of the pessimistic scenario coming true. Again, take in the gut reaction that rejects the possibility that in 1 out of 4 possible worlds, we'll be dealing with COVID-19 through 2027 or even later. It feels repugnant.

Here, it might help to remember the words shared by billionaire Ray Dalio, head of the well-known Bridgewater Associates fund, which manages about $160 billion in global investments, about COVID-19 in a March 3 LinkedIn post: "The most important assets that you need to take good care of are you and your family. As with investing, I hope that you will imagine the worst-case scenario and protect yourself against it." See this scenario as the realistic pessimistic scenario – it might happen, after all – and take the steps needed to protect yourself, your household, your career, and your organization.

After that, consider what kind of information would lead you to believe each of these scenarios is taking place, ranging from reports from experts on vaccines to local investigative journalists uncovering government incompetence. As you go forward, monitor these sources of information to see what future you're actually going toward, and adjust your plans accordingly to address problems, seize opportunities, and reserve appropriate resources.

DO NOT simply hope for the optimistic scenario. There's an insightful phrase attributed to Vince Lombardi, "Hope is not a strategy," and you don't want to rely on hope.

Of course, the likely reality would be some hodgepodge of these scenarios, and we're only considering two factors, the ones of most relevance to the pandemic. You'll probably want to explore other factors and other scenarios relevant to your situation.

Next, the "Defend Your Future" technique involves imagining what your life or business would look like in the next five years in each of these scenarios. Doing so will help you solve problems, seize opportunities, and invest resources wisely.

Defend Your Future: Solve Problems, Seize Opportunities, Invest Resources

First, gather the people relevant to the planning process, whether it's the leadership team of your business or other organization, or the members of your household, no more than 10 people and ideally no more than six. For household decision-making, include older children so that they have buy-in into the eventual plan outcomes. For organizations, consider recruiting an independent facilitator who is not part of the team to help guide the exercise, to prevent personality issues, power dynamics, and bias blind spots from damaging your eventual plan. If you're individually working on your career plan, make sure to get either an external perspective on your process while you're working through this exercise, or at least on the outcomes of the exercise, to address dangerous judgment errors.

Next, determine what your plan would look like for each of the three future scenarios. Work one by one through each of the areas described in the previous chapters.

For households, that includes: 1) Safety; 2) Connection; 3) Self-Esteem; 4) Exploration; 5) Love toward others; 6) Purpose.

For organizations, that includes transforming your internal business model: 1) Motivation and engagement; 2) Effective communication; 3) Noticing and solving problems and conflicts; 4) Cultivating trust; 5) Security; 6) Accountability. And don't forget your external business model: 1) Deliver offerings virtually; 2) Cultivate relationships virtually; 3) Manage external stakeholder disruptions; 4) Anticipate socioeconomic shifts; 5) Prepare for unknown unknowns; 6) Outcompete your competition.

Now, brainstorm what possible problems might arise internally to your organization, household, or career that might undermine your plan. If you're doing this as a group – whether organization or household – start by having everyone write out ANONYMOUSLY all the possible problems that might arise, including low-probability ones.

Anonymity is critically important to avoid several problems that typically accompany group decision-making. First, the phenomenon of groupthink, when everyone forms a consensus opinion based on the prevailing opinion of people with authority in the room. Second, the shoot-the-messenger or mum effect, the tendency to avoid revealing bad news to those in positions of power, for fear of being associated with negative information by those with authority.

The next step involves evaluating the problems. Discuss the likelihood that it might occur and the kind and amount of resources (money, time, information, social capital, strategic planning) that might be needed to address it in each scenario. Try to convert the resources into money if possible in order to have a single unit of measurement. After discussing each problem, have everyone anonymously write out their estimate of the probability and resource demands of each problem, and average out the differences.

Multiply the average probability by resource amount to get a final anticipated estimate of each problem's impact. For example, if your leadership team estimates a 27% probability of a COVID-19 outbreak among the employees in your business per year if you try to maintain an in-office setting at a cost to your productivity and healthcare expenses of $370,000, that occurrence would be a total anticipated impact of $99,900 per year.

Next consider what you can do to address the internal problems in advance, and write out how much you anticipate these steps might cost. As always, first discuss, and then have everyone write out their final estimates anonymously.

For instance, your team might decide that one option is to take extensive sanitation, social distancing, and working in shifts measures that would cost $37,000 per year, and decrease the probability of an outbreak by 60%, so the estimated impact would be decreased from $99,900 to $39,960. In that case, the total expected cost to your business would be $79,960 per year, instead of $99,900 per year, a saving of nearly $20,000.

Your team might decide that the other option would be to switch to a fully virtual team. It would cost about $24,000 to terminate your current lease agreement, and free up the $13,600 per month you're currently paying for office space and related expenses for in-person office space, for a saving of $139,200 the first year and $163,200 from then on. The switch would be accompanied by all the costs in providing support for employees working at home, from professional development to cybersecurity, including funding for co-working spaces for employees who need to be surrounded by others in their work. You'd also deal with lost productivity at least in the short and medium term and may lose a couple of employees constitutionally incapable of making this switch. Overall, they estimate the cost to transition in the first year would be $113,000, followed by ongoing costs of $58,000 per year.

That's a bargain, considering how much you'd be saving by not paying for office space and related expenses, not even including how much you'd save by protecting your employees from an outbreak. It makes much more sense for you to switch to virtual teams rather than trying to continue in-office work, and you might decide to go that way as a means of solving this problem.

Finally, add up all the extra resources that may be needed due to the various possible internal problems and/or all the steps you committed to taking to address them in advance. Make sure to do so for all three scenarios.

Next, take the same steps as above, but for external problems rather than internal ones (again, ensuring anonymity at key points). A case in point, you may consider the likelihood of unwise decision-making by government officials, disruptions among your supply chains, major investors running out of funding, and other issues relevant to you. If you're planning for a household, you might evaluate the possibility of needing to support relatives who aren't part of your household and made unwise decisions due to excessive optimism about the length and impact of the pandemic and similar issues.

Following that, go on to opportunities, internal and external, and repeat the same steps. For example, an internal opportunity might be for team members to work in a more flexible manner that fits their scheduling better. Such flexibility, research shows, helps promote employee retention and engagement. Just designate an obligatory time when everyone has to be available – say 12 to 3PM – to help ensure coordination and collaboration, and you'll be set. An external opportunity might be for your previously in-person sales team to learn quickly how to do effective virtual sales and expand its range of prospects beyond previous geographical restrictions.

As the final step, decide what scenario you will target initially. I urge you to land somewhere between the moderate and pessimistic scenario. Remember that hope is not a strategy, so prepare for the more pessimistic case, while hoping for the most optimistic one. Think of it like insurance: insure yourself for worse than average government (in)competence, both in balancing economic and health concerns and bringing an effective vaccine into wide use.

Go back to the adjustments to your plans you made to account for threats and opportunities going into this scenario, and add them into your plan of actions. Likewise, add up all the resources you decided to invest, ideally expressed in money but also in other forms – information, time, and social capital – and prepare to acquire/reserve them as needed.

Defend Your Future: Check for Cognitive Biases

After you've figured out your initial draft of threats, opportunities, and resources, you need to check for cognitive biases. Address both ones that are particularly problematic in the context of COVID-19 and ones that are relevant to planning more broadly.

The normalcy bias: Have you truly adjusted for the reality of the pandemic? Our autopilot system finds it incredibly hard to do so. Even I'm still struggling with doing so, despite all my work helping clients adapt to our new abnormal, as well as my media interviews and the writing of this book.

A helpful exercise involves walking yourself or your leadership team through what you anticipate a typical day might look like a year from now. What will you do as you start your (work)day? How will you collaborate with others on projects inside your company (household)? What about how you will reach out to and cultivate external stakeholders? What might be on the nightly business news in that realistic pessimistic scenario for which you're preparing? Now go back to your plans, and see if you need to make any adjustments.

The attentional bias: How might the last couple of articles you read about COVID-19 be influencing your planning? For example, on the prominent libertarian website Reason.com, which I and a number of my clients enjoy, the most popular article on April 17, 2020 was called "COVID-19 Lethality Not Much Different Than Flu, Says New Study." The article reported on the results of a study, which was not peer reviewed, using Facebook to solicit residents of Santa Clara County, California to get antibody tests for COVID-19. Based on those antibody tests, the researchers then estimated the total infection and fatality rate of COVID-19 as .12-.2%, much lower than the prevalent estimates at the time and slightly higher than the fatality rate of the flu.

The upshot of the article was this phrase: "Assuming that their findings are happily confirmed, among the important public benefits would be a quicker end to the pandemic lockdown we are all experiencing." That phrase reveals the journalist's motivation in reporting on this study: he wanted to use it as a blow for the end of government lockdowns. It would work fine as an opinion piece, and quite appropriately for a libertarian venue, but it's journalistic malpractice to report on it as a straightforward news story.

First, the journalist failed to state clearly that the study very much represents an outlier in terms of its findings. Moreover, he failed to share that the study doesn't claim that the numbers actually represent the true fatality rate across the country.

Since the subjects were solicited via Facebook, the study did not have a representative sample of the population. Instead, as the study itself said, "our sampling strategy selected for members of Santa Clara County with access to Facebook and a car to attend drive-through testing sites. This resulted in an overrepresentation of white women between the ages of 19 and 64."

Guess what? The fatality rate in COVID-19, according to a wide variety of quality, peer-reviewed studies, is substantially higher for men than for women, and more importantly for people 60 and above. Most of the deaths occur for people over 60. Indeed, the deadliest clusters of COVID-19 happened in nursing homes, which combine older adults with lack of social distancing.

Just as importantly, the main problem with COVID-19 doesn't come from the base fatality rate that you get when you only have a few cases and can provide them with top-notch treatment: Santa Clara County had only 32 deaths when the study was conducted. The biggest challenge comes from when you don't control outbreaks and then your health system gets overwhelmed, as happened in Wuhan, New York, Northern Italy, and elsewhere. That's the main goal of shutdowns and social distancing.

The journalist, of course, knew this, and deliberately chose to ignore this information for his ideological ends. That article made me quite a bit more suspicious of articles on Reason.com on similar topics, and I began to treat them more as opinion pieces than quality journalism.

Reflect on whether and how what you've been reading, watching, or listening to lately might have influenced your attention and evaluation, and adjust your plans accordingly.

Anchoring: Recall how you perceived the COVID-19 situation before you started reading this book. It's hard for us to update appropriately based on new information; we tend to stick to our preexisting positions too much.

While appropriate for many situations, this gut reaction is a poor fit for slow-moving, high-impact, low-probability train wrecks like a pandemic. This kind of catastrophe, as you know by now, triggers a series of cognitive biases that result in systematically bad decision-making and information sharing by politicians, business leaders, journalists, and other authority figures. As a result, it's very likely that a great deal of information you received had a problematic slant, even without any intentional spin such as by the Reason.com journalist. Do your best to set it aside, and go back to reevaluate your plan with a fresh perspective.

Hyperbolic discounting: It's challenging for us to avoid short-termism and sufficiently value the long-term. Here's a helpful activity to do so.

Imagine yourself five years from now, stuck with the results of whatever plan you made today. Really, truly put yourself into the shoes of yourself in five years. Think about where you'd be in your business, what you'd be focusing on, what you'd look like: consider using one of those aging apps to age yourself by five years (not FaceApp, it steals your data).

Then, put yourself into the role of your older self, and send a message – e-mail, voicemail, video recording to your current self. Make sure to share what your current self did well, and what they could have done better in their planning. Now, use that message to go back to your plan and change it in such a way as to better fit the needs of yourself five years from now.

The planning fallacy: Our excessive confidence in everything going according to plan, and reluctance to either build in enough additional resources to address risks and problems, or to pivot quickly enough when needed to adjust to new conditions.

Think back to your past plans. When they went wrong, how did they go wrong? Did you spend too little time gathering information before making your move and ran into an unanticipated risk, or too much time and wasted an excellent opportunity? Did you stick too long with a failing business partnership, or cut your relationships too quickly when they still could have been salvaged? Go back and revise your plans so as to address typical patterns of dangerous judgment errors that you tend to commit the most.

The overconfidence bias: We're way too confident about our judgments. As a result, we make too many snap decisions and go for the first viable option even in important decisions when we should develop several viable alternatives.

In planning, this tendency comes through most clearly when we're deciding on the ways that we'll address threats and take advantage of opportunities. The first answer that comes to mind is very frequently far from the best option. So go back to your plan and revisit how you intend to solve problems and seize opportunities. Evaluate whether there are other viable options to doing so than what you've considered so far, and whether you should replace your current solutions with these new ones.

Optimism bias: If you're in a leadership role in a business, you're most likely too optimistic about the market conditions and the prospects for your business. In fact, studies show that most Americans tend to be too optimistic, and those in leadership positions even more so.

If you know yourself to be in that majority, take a few minutes to look at the dark side of life. Imagine that things go worse for your business than you hope. What if the pessimistic scenario occurs? Or what if the moderate case occurs, but you suffer a severe case of COVID-19, as happened to my dad, taking you out of commission for six weeks? Ruminate on that dark side, and then go back to your plan and see if there are any adjustments needed.

Confirmation bias: Our predilection to look for whatever supports our preexisting perspective, and ignore even accurate information that doesn't do so. What's your existing framework of looking at the world? Who are your role models and sources of authority? How do you think about other people's motivations and incentives, their needs and drivers?

What do you believe about the appropriate role of government intervention in the economy during health challenges? More importantly, what do you believe regional government officials will do in the course of the pandemic? After all, it doesn't matter much what you believe from the perspective of what will happen. We too often make the mistake of weighing our opinion excessively. The key for government action is what those who lead your national and regional government believe: can you model them well?

Try your best to envision the world from an alternative perspective. What if the opposite was true for each of the questions posed above: your role models are wrong, your perception of other people is broken, your perspective on the government's role is off base. How would you change your plans and activities with that in mind? Now go back to your plan, and see if it needs any revisions.

Bias blind spot: This is for those who didn't make any revisions in your plans after the previous prompts – it's our tendency to believe we don't suffer from biases. Heck, after writing out this exercise and reminding myself of the prompts, I went back and tweaked some of the plans for my own consulting, coaching, and training business pivoting to delivering its services fully online.

I'd be shocked if you didn't need to make any revisions. If you indeed failed to make changes, you're very likely falling for the bias blind spot. It's time to go back and reread the cognitive biases from the start, and revise your plans once again.

If you are planning this out as a team, discuss the cognitive biases, then come up with resource amount adjustments ANONYMOUSLY, and average out the differences.

Defend Your Future: Unknown Unknowns

Next, address potential unknown unknowns, and especially high-impact black swans, in your plan. Scan all of your scenarios for potential major disruptors.

Some might be due to COVID-19 itself. For instance, it's well known that the first wave of the 1918 Spanish flu, while highly contagious, was only about as deadly as the regular flu, killing .1% of those infected. However, the virus mutated in the summer of 1918 to become much more deadly, capable of killing a healthy person within 24 hours of first showing signs of infection. It now had a mortality rate of 2.5-5%, so 25 times more deadly than the regular flu and 5 times more deadly than COVID-19. One potential horrific black swan would be COVID-19 mutating to become as or more deadly than the Spanish flu, while retaining its previous high contagiousness. What would you do in response to that terrible scenario?

Other major disruptors might come from the consequences of

COVID-19. Imagine that government incompetence dealing with the pandemic and consequent infighting among political leaders led to growing civil unrest and the eventual cancellation of the US November election. How would the resulting constitutional crisis and civil strife impact you?

A third set of major disruptors might have nothing to do with COVID-19 directly. For instance, early 2020 saw East Africa experience its worst wave of locusts in decades, due to unusually heavy rains that resulted from climate change. These voracious pests devoured basic food crops across Kenya, Ethiopia, Somalia, and other countries in the Horn of Africa. While not resulting directly from COVID-19, the pandemic makes the locusts much harder to control, due to a combination of shutdowns, social distancing, travel restrictions, and supply chain disruptions. Moreover, wealthy countries, focused on COVID-19, did not provide the typical humanitarian aid they would provide in such situations.

If your business depended on supply chains in those countries, it would be majorly disrupted. Scan for similar possibilities, where COVID-19 might not lead to the disruption, but exacerbate it, especially due to the growing climate change-caused disruptions around the world. For example, might an abnormally intense hurricane season combine with difficulty preparing for and mitigating the consequences of such events due to the novel coronavirus? What about floods, wildfires, or tornadoes? For a non-climate change related event, how about a major earthquake.

Let's not forget human-caused disruption, whether from stupidity, ignorance, or maliciousness. A case in point of the latter might be a group of terrorists taking advantage of everyone's growing reliance on digital technology to cope with COVID-19 to launch a series of cyberattacks on services that have grown critically important in this pandemic, ranging from Amazon to Slack to Microsoft Teams.

It's time to go back to your plan and adjust it to account for these disruptors. Add the resources you think are needed to deal with them.

After you do so, recognize that this process helped you address grey swans, since you've now turned some black swans into grey ones by recognizing the possibility of their existence. You also need to account for true black swans, things that you can't address because you genuinely don't know they can happen or are completely unpredictable.

To help you prepare for true black swans, double the resources that you added for the grey swans. Many of my clients buck at doing so, as it seems excessive. I encourage them to imagine how much better off they'd be if they had a cushion to address past disruptors, remind them about the normalcy bias, and underscore that simply hoping nothing truly bad happens isn't a strategy. Those reminders help them get over the hump.

Defend Your Future: Communicate and Take Next Steps

Next, communicate effectively about this planning exercise to key stakeholders. When doing so, highlight in particular the need to reserve and invest needed resources. Many people feel surprised when they learn how much resources they actually need to reserve to protect themselves and their business. You'll need to show them how and why you made your decisions in developing and adjusting your plan to get their buy-in on plan implementation.

Finally, execute! Take the next steps that you decided on during this exercise to address unanticipated problems and take advantage of opportunities, and reserving the resources to do so. Monitor the information you chose to determine which future you're heading toward, adjusting your plan, activities, and resource reserve as needed. Be ready to pivot as needed based on the evidence, updating your beliefs quickly and avoiding the many cognitive biases plaguing our planning, especially in the context of major disruption.

In the next chapter, we'll turn to making major decisions as you develop your plans. In the meantime, to get a thorough workbook on going through the "Defend Your Future" technique, along with a recorded webinar and the most up-to-date evidence about adapting and planning most effectively for COVID-19, please visit https://disasteravoidanceexperts.com/adapt.

Chapter 5

Making the Best Major Decisions

When making your plan, you might come across the need to make a major decision. Or perhaps you're thinking about a major decision you want to make right now, even before you start developing your plan. Here's an 8-step process to do so, in a way that addresses a large number of cognitive biases at once.

8 Steps to Making the Best Major Decisions

Step 1: Identify the need to launch a decision-making process. Such recognition bears particular weight when there's no explicit crisis that cries out for a decision to be made or when your natural intuitions make it uncomfortable to acknowledge the need for a tough decision. The best decision makers take initiative to recognize the need for decisions before they become an emergency and don't let gut reactions cloud their decision-making capacity.

Step 2: Gather relevant information from a wide variety of informed perspectives on the issue at hand. Value especially those opinions with which you disagree. Contradicting perspectives empower you to distance yourself from the comfortable reliance on your gut instincts and help you recognize any potential bias blind spots.

Step 3: With the data gathered, decide the goals you want to reach. Painting a clear vision of the desired outcome of your decision-making process. It's particularly important to recognize when a seemingly one-time decision is a symptom of an underlying issue with processes and practices. Make addressing these root problems part of the outcome you want to achieve.

Step 4: Develop a clear decision-making process criteria to weigh the various options of how you'd like to get to your vision. If at all possible, develop these criteria before you start to consider choices. Our intuitions bias our decision-making criteria to encourage certain outcomes that fit our instincts. As a result, you get overall worse decisions if you don't develop criteria before starting to look at options. Rank the importance of each criteria on a scale of 1 (low) to 10 (high).

Step 5: Generate a number of viable options that can achieve your decision-making process goals. We frequently fall into the trap of generating insufficient options to make the best decisions, especially for solving underlying challenges. To address this, it's very important to generate many more options that seem intuitive to us. Otherwise, we tend to generate only one or at most two options, and go with the one we initially prefer, rather than truly considering the variety of possible futures to make the most effective choice. Go for five attractive options as the minimum. Remember that this is a brainstorming step, so don't judge options, even though they might seem outlandish or politically unacceptable. In my consulting and coaching experience, the optimal choice often involves elements drawn from out-of-the-box and innovative options.

Step 6: Weigh these options, picking the best of the bunch. When weighing options, beware of going with your initial preferences, and do your best to see your own preferred choice in a harsh light. Moreover, do your best to evaluate each option separately from your opinion of the person who proposed it, to minimize the impact of personalities, relationships, and internal politics on the decision itself.

Step 7: Implement the option you chose. For implementing the decision, you need to minimize risks and maximize rewards, since your goal is to get a decision outcome that's as good as possible. First, imagine the decision completely fails. Then, brainstorm about all the problems that led to this failure. Next, consider how you might solve these problems, and integrate the solutions into your implementation plan. Then, imagine the decision absolutely succeeded. Brainstorm all the reasons for success, consider how you can bring these reasons into life, and integrate what you learned into implementing the decisions. If you're doing this as part of a team, ensure clear accountability and communication around the decision's enactment.

Step 8: Evaluate the implementation of the decision and revise as needed. As part of your implementation plan, develop clear metrics of success that you can measure throughout the implementation process. Check in regularly to ensure the implementation is meeting or exceeding its success metrics. If it's not, revise the implementation as needed. Sometimes, you'll realize you need to revise the original decision as well, and that's fine, just go back to the step that you need to revise and proceed from that step again.

More broadly, you'll often find yourself going back and forth among these steps. Doing so is an inherent part of making a significant decision, and does not indicate a problem in your process. For example, say you're at the option-generation stage, and you discover relevant new information. You might need to go back and revise the goals and criteria stages.

Making the Best Decisions: A Pandemic Case Study

Due to the devastating impact of the COVID-19 pandemic on the restaurant industry, one of my coaching clients, Alex, who served as the Chief Operating Officer (COO) in a regional chain of 24 diners in the Northeast US, wanted to explore switching her career to a different industry. The restaurants had shifted to a takeout model, but faced mounting losses, and the government bailout, she thought, might not save the chain if the pandemic lasted for more than a few months. She felt worried about the very high probability of having to shift to a lower-ranking role in order to get into a new industry, but also worried about her future if she stuck to the restaurant industry.

She turned to me as her executive coach and asked for guidance. I recommended this exercise, and coached her through the steps.

Step 1: She already decided to evaluate the decision to switch, so there was nothing further here.

Step 2: I asked Alex to gather information from a wide variety of people with relevant perspectives. They included professional colleagues and mentors in the restaurant industry; contacts in other industries such as vendors to her restaurant chain; experts on the pandemic; and family members impacted by her potential switch, especially her stay-at-home husband who took care of her kids.

In particular, I urged her to include input from executives in her network who shifted to another industry, both those who made the switch successfully and those who did not. Likewise, I encouraged her to have a serious conversation with her accountant on her financial capacity to bear a job search that might take a long time, given the tribulations and uncertainty caused by the pandemic.

Step 3: With the data she had on hand, I asked Alex to come up with a list of critical goals, which should address underlying issues as well. Among the goals identified were:

- To make sure that within a year, she had a role that would pay her at least 75% of the salary that she was getting as COO of the restaurant chain, whether by staying at the chain or switching to another industry, per her accountant's guidance.

- To ensure that she had substantial room for career growth if she did make the switch.

One underlying issue that Alex identified is that while she favored innovation in business, she was often at loggerheads with several key stakeholders in her current company who didn't want to deviate from traditional business methods. She was hoping that in shifting to a different industry and company, she would be able to address this issue as well. So an additional goal was to enable her to satisfy her passion for innovation.

Step 4: Alex came up with a number of criteria relevant for the switch and ranked them on her priorities, with 1 at the low end and 10 at the high end:

- Salary in a year (8)
- Innovation opportunity (5)
- Room for growth (6)
- Stability for the industry and the company in the foreseeable medium and long-term future (7)
- Ease of transition (5)

Step 5: Initially, Alex listed just one option for switching: it was obvious that she was already leaning towards the food delivery industry. However, I convinced her to add three more options so that she would have five at the minimum. She took a bit more time deliberating and finally came up with five options:

- Stay in her current position
- Food delivery industry

- Meal kit industry
- Food processing industry
- Grocery store industry

Step 6: At this point, Alex was still leaning towards her favored option, which was to shift to the food delivery industry. She informed me that some of her former colleagues were also able to easily transition to this industry. However, I cautioned her to consider and evaluate each option carefully, and separate each option from those who recommended it to her. I also urged her to factor in all the variables first, such as the fact that the grocery store industry was booming and will continue to do so. So we went together through each option, and she ranked each option on each criteria variable. To do so, we made a table with options on the left and variables on the top. Then, after ranking each option on the relevant criteria, we multiplied the ranking by the weight of the criteria.

Options	Salary (8)	Innovation (5)	Room for growth (6)	Stability (7)	Ease of transition (5)	Total
Current position	7	1	2	1	10	130
Food delivery	5	3	4	4	8	147
Meal Kit	5	7	4	3	3	135
Food processing	6	2	5	5	3	138
Grocery store	8	5	9	8	5	224

Table used by Alex to calculate her preferred industries.

She was very surprised to discover that the grocery store option proved much better than all the other ones, including her favored food delivery option. That's because grocery stores boomed due to the pandemic, and were hiring both workers and executives left and right.

Moreover, those with whom she spoke foresaw that the pandemic would lead to lasting changes in how people got food, with a much bigger emphasis on eating at home and much less on either restaurants or cafeterias in the workplace. Given that people had more time than before, and looked for ways to occupy themselves, they also foresaw a shift away from delivery and meal kits, with more people spending their time cooking instead.

The grocery store industry thus offered much more room for growth, stability, and salary potential than the other fields she considered. Due to their extensive hiring, she judged it not too difficult to transition there. Due to the many options within grocery stores, they had significant room for innovation as well.

Step 7: I guided Alex through the step of imagining a decision failure. Alex imagined that the switch to the grocery store industry failed because of three things:

- Lack of proper network with which to source for possible job opportunities.
- Unwillingness to take on a role that is a step down in the organizational hierarchy.
- Inflexible attitude when learning new things, brought about by years of calling the shots as COO.

Alex realized that while she had an extensive network, most of the professional contacts she had cultivated were from the restaurant industry, so her network might not be adequate for job hunting. She also had some reservations about having to take a lower-ranking role, considering how hard and how long she had worked in order to become a COO. Finally, she contemplated how difficult it might be to have to relinquish being in the driver's seat and follow someone else's business strategy if she does step into a non-COO role.

Alex brainstormed on possible solutions and decided on the following:

- Spend a month growing her network so that she could make new contacts and get to know key players in the grocery store industry.
- Get in touch with former colleagues and mentors who had stepped down from top leadership roles to get their advice and insight on what they learned from the experience.
- Upon landing a good role, focus on learning new skills, brushing up on old ones, and doing a deep dive to get to know the grocery food industry. This way, she could focus her attention on becoming a valuable member of senior management instead of dwelling on any "power limitations."

When she had finished imagining failure and brainstorming for solutions, Alex proceeded to imagine that the decision to shift to a new role and industry was a success. After thinking of potential reasons for this success, Alex determined that this was largely due to her efforts to efficiently transition to her new role and industry by building new core skills. Aside from this, she was also able to bring some of her unique skills from the restaurant industry to the grocery store industry, including:

- Knowing how to serve customers effectively through creating a positive customer experience.
- Her expertise in managing prepared food delivery, which was a crucial skill to have, given that grocery stores had to deliver food extensively during the pandemic.
- Extensive knowledge on how supply chains operate, a strategic skill to have since the grocery store industry also faces issues of supply chain disruptions due to the pandemic.

Step 8: Alex was eventually able to successfully shift industries. Within six weeks, she was able to get into a large grocery chain as Senior Vice President of Prepared Foods. While it was a step down from her role as COO, she was able to get a compensation package that was 85% of what she received as COO in her former company, owing to the fact that she had joined a much larger organization in a booming industry. I guided Alex through the implementation of her decision, where she set the following metrics of success:

- Expand her network by adding 6 contacts/month specifically from the grocery store industry.
- Identify and work on 4 core skills that she needed in order to thrive in her new role and industry.
- Identify at least 6 key people in her new network and engage with them every two weeks on specific industry issues.
- Develop mentors within this new industry.

Using this technique, you can make the best decisions, whether as an individual or organization, on any major issue. Make sure to get a workbook on going through the "Making the Best Major Decisions" technique, as well as a recorded webinar and updated information on adapting and planning for COVID-19, at https://disasteravoidanceexperts.com/adapt.

Conclusion:

Survive and Thrive in the New Abnormal

The world is moving at a lightning-fast pace, and you don't have all day to get to the actual process of adapting and planning after doing the reading if you are to survive and thrive. You now have all the tools you need to do so.

You now know about the most important cognitive biases you need to avoid in making decisions on how to evaluate, adapt to, and plan for the pandemic: normalcy bias; attentional bias; anchoring; hyperbolic discounting; planning fallacy; overconfidence bias; optimism bias; confirmation bias; bias blind spot. You are aware of the key needs for adapting as individuals for your households and careers: safety; connection; self-esteem; exploration; love for others; purpose. You also understand the need to adapt your organization by fundamentally transforming your business model, internal and external, for virtual collaboration and service delivery. Finally, you have the "Defend Your Future" technique to make your strategic long-term plan for an uncertain future of a number of potential scenarios, and can use the "Make the Best Decisions" technique when you reach a critical decision point.

Remember that these insights will be applicable not only to the COVID-19 pandemic, but to all high-impact disasters, especially slow-moving ones. The "Defend Your Future" and "Make the Best Decisions" techniques, with a few minor revisions, can be used easily to make strategic plans and major decisions in a time of peace and plenty, as well as a time of turbulence and tribulations. Keep this book handy and reread it as you make your way through the challenges of the pandemic and emerge, eventually, into the post-pandemic society, and keep using the insights from it to tweak your activities, plans, and decisions.

By following these guidelines, I feel confident you will maximize your chances of being on the right side of history, and will be counted among the winners by historians writing the history books. And remember that history is written by the winners, so your savvy and creative navigation of the major disruption of the pandemic may well wind up in those books.

I'm eager to hear how you used the techniques in the book and how they impacted your life and work. Leave your thoughts in a book review on Amazon.com and Goodreads.com, and get in touch with me to share your thoughts or ask any questions at Gleb@DisasterAvoidanceExperts.com. Remember that there's a workbook on going through the "Defend Your Future" and the "Making the Best Decisions" techniques, a number of other resources such as a recorded webinar, and detailed and updated information reflecting the latest findings on adapting and planning most effectively for COVID-19 at https://disasteravoidanceexperts.com/adapt.

Bibliography

Note: Due to the constantly evolving science on the novel coronavirus, and the multitude of pre-prints of journal articles which I consulted, I will not be including my research in the bibliography. Suffice to say it was extensive and exhaustive of the currently-available material in the English language at the time of the publication of this book. Instead, the bibliography will focus on books and articles relevant to cognitive biases and decision-making strategies, with the aim of helping readers who want to explore this field in more depth.

Chapter 1

Ariely, Dan. *Predictably irrational*. New York: HarperCollins, 2008.

Banaji, Mahzarin R., and Anthony G. Greenwald. *Blindspot: Hidden biases of good people*. New York: Bantam, 2016.

Buehler, Roger, Dale Griffin, and Michael Ross. "Inside the Planning Fallacy: The Causes and Consequences of Optimistic Time Predictions." In Gilovich, Thomas, Dale Griffin, and Daniel Kahneman, eds. *Heuristics and Biases: The Psychology of Intuitive Judgment*. Cambridge, UK: Cambridge University Press, 2002.

Del Giudice, Marco. *Evolutionary Psychopathology: A Unified Approach*. Oxford, UK: Oxford University Press, 2018.

Dobelli, Rolf. *The Art of Thinking Clearly: Better Thinking, Better Decisions*. London: Hachette UK, 2013.

Fox, Elaine, Riccardo Russo, and Kevin Dutton. "Attentional Bias for Threat: Evidence for Delayed Disengagement from Emotional Faces." *Cognition and Emotion* 16, no. 3 (2002): 355-379.

Gigerenzer, Gerd. *Gut Feelings: The Intelligence of the Unconscious*. New York: Penguin, 2007.

Gigerenzer, Gerd, and Reinhard Selten, eds. *Bounded Rationality: The Adaptive Toolbox*. Cambridge, MA: MIT Press, 2002.

Kahneman, Daniel, and Patrick Egan. *Thinking, Fast and Slow*. Vol. 1. New York: Farrar, Straus and Giroux, 2011.

Laibson, David. "Golden Eggs and Hyperbolic Discounting." *The Quarterly Journal of Economics* 112, no. 2 (1997): 443-478.

Omer, Haim, and Nahman Alon. "The continuity principle: A unified approach to disaster and trauma." *American Journal of Community Psychology* 22, no. 2 (1994): 273-287.

Sanna, Lawrence J., Craig D. Parks, Edward C. Chang, and Seth E. Carter. "The Hourglass Is Half Full or Half Empty: Temporal Framing and the Group Planning Fallacy." *Group Dynamics: Theory, Research, and Practice* 9, no. 3 (2005): 173-188.

Stanovich, Keith. *Rationality and the Reflective Mind*. Oxford, UK: Oxford University Press, 2011.

Strack, Fritz, and Thomas Mussweiler. "Explaining the enigmatic anchoring effect: Mechanisms of selective accessibility." *Journal of Personality and Social Psychology* 73, no. 3 (1997): 437-446.

Tedlow, Richard S. *Denial: Why Business Leaders Fail to Look Facts in the Face – and What to Do About It*. New York: Penguin, 2010.

Thaler, Richard H. *Nudge: Improving Decisions About Health, Wealth, and Happiness*. New Haven, CT: Yale University Press, 2008.

Tsipursky, Gleb. *Never Go With Your Gut: How Pioneering Leaders Make the Best Decisions and Avoid Business Disasters*. Newburyport, MA: Career Press, 2019.

Tsipursky, Gleb. *The Truth-Seeker's Handbook: A Science-Based Guide*. Columbus, OH: Intentional Insights, 2017.

Yamori, K. "Revisiting the concept of normalcy bias." *Japanese Journal of Experimental Social Psychology* 48, no. 2 (2009): 137-149.

Chapter 2

Haidt, Jonathan. *The Happiness Hypothesis: Putting Ancient Wisdom and Philosophy to the Test of Modern Science.* London: Arrow, 2007.

Kaufman, Scott Barry. *Transcend: The New Science of Self-Actualization.* New York: TarcherPerigee, 2020.

Tsipursky, Gleb. *Find Your Purpose Using Science.* Columbus: Intentional Insights, 2015.

Tsipursky, Gleb. *The Blindspots Between Us: How to Overcome Unconscious Cognitive Bias & Build Better Relationships.* Oakland, CA: New Harbinger, 2020.

Tsipursky, Gleb, and Fabio Votta. "Fighting Fake News and Post-Truth Politics with Behavioral Science: The Pro-Truth Pledge." *Behavior and Social Issues* 27, no. 2 (2018): 47-70.

Tsipursky, Gleb, Fabio Votta, and James Mulick. "Fighting Fake News with Psychology. The Pro-Truth Pledge." *Journal of Social and Political Psychology* 6, no. 2 (2018): 271-290.

Tsipursky, Gleb, and Zachary Morford. "Addressing Behaviors That Lead to Sharing Fake News." *Behavior and Social Issues* 27 (2018): 6-10.

Tsipursky, Gleb and Tim Ward. *Pro Truth: A Practical Plan for Putting Truth Back into Politics.* Washington, DC: Changemakers Books, 2020.

Chapter 3

Taleb, Nasim N. *The Black Swan: The Impact of the Highly Improbable.* New York: Random House, 2007.

Chapter 4

Aczel, Balazs, Bence Bago, Aba Szollosi, Andrei Foldes, and Bence Lukacs. "Is it time for studying real-life debiasing? Evaluation of the effectiveness of an analogical intervention technique." *Frontiers in Psychology* 6 (2015): 1-13.

Almashat, Sammy, Brian Ayotte, Barry Edelstein, and Jennifer

Margrett. "Framing effect debiasing in medical decision making." *Patient Education and Counseling* 71, no. 1 (2008): 102-107.

Bhandari, Gokul, Khaled Hassanein, and Richard Deaves. "Debiasing investors with decision support systems: An experimental investigation." *Decision Support Systems* 46, no. 1 (2008): 399-410.

Croskerry, Pat. "When I say... cognitive debiasing." *Medical Education* 49, no. 7 (2015): 656-657.

Croskerry, Pat, Geeta Singhal, and Sílvia Mamede. "Cognitive debiasing 1: origins of bias and theory of debiasing." *BMJ Quality and Safety* (2013): 1-7.

Gallop, David, Chris Willy, and John Bischoff. "How to catch a black swan: Measuring the benefits of the premortem technique for risk identification." *Journal of Enterprise Transformation* 6, no. 2 (2016): 87-106.

Graf, Lorenz, Andreas König, Albrecht Enders, and Harald Hungenberg. "Debiasing competitive irrationality: How managers can be prevented from trading off absolute for relative profit." *European Management Journal* 30, no. 4 (2012): 386-403.

Heath, Chip, and Dan Heath. *Decisive: How to Make Better Choices in Life and Work.* New York: Random House, 2013.

Heath, Chip, and Dan Heath. *Switch: How to Change Things When Change Is Hard.* New York: Crown Business, 2010.

Kahneman, Daniel, and Dan Lovallo. "Delusions of success: How optimism undermines executives' decisions." *Harvard Business Review* 81, no. 7 (2003): 56-63.

Kaustia, Markku, and Milla Perttula. "Overconfidence and debiasing in the financial industry." *Review of Behavioral Finance* 4, no. 1 (2012): 46-62.

Lewandowsky, Stephan, Ullrich KH Ecker, Colleen M. Seifert, Norbert Schwarz, and John Cook. "Misinformation and Its Correction: Continued Influence and Successful Debiasing."

Psychological Science in the Public Interest 13, no. 3 (2012): 106-131.

Lilienfeld, Scott O., Rachel Ammirati, and Kristin Landfield. "Giving Debiasing Away: Can Psychological Research on Correcting Cognitive Errors Promote Human Welfare?" *Perspectives on Psychological Science* 4, no. 4 (2009): 390-398.

Mahajan, Jayashree. "The Overconfidence Effect in Marketing Management Predictions." *Journal of Marketing Research* 29, no. 3 (1992): 329-342.

Meissner, Philip, and Torsten Wulf. "The development of strategy scenarios based on prospective hindsight." *Journal of Strategy and Management* (2015).

Morewedge, Carey K., Haewon Yoon, Irene Scopelliti, Carl W. Symborski, James H. Korris, and Karim S. Kassam. "Debiasing Decisions: Improved Decision Making With a Single Training Intervention." *Policy Insights from the Behavioral and Brain Sciences* 2, no. 1 (2015): 129-140.

Nickerson, Raymond S. "Confirmation Bias: A Ubiquitous Phenomenon in Many Guises." *Review of General Psychology* 2, no. 2 (1998): 175-220.

Rose, Jason P. "Debiasing comparative optimism and increasing worry for health outcomes." *Journal of Health Psychology* 17, no. 8 (2012): 1121-1131.

Rosen, Sidney, and Abraham Tesser. "On Reluctance to Communicate Undesirable Information: The MUM effect." *Sociometry* (1970): 253-263.

Tetlock, Philip E. *Expert Political Judgment: How good is it? How can we know?* Princeton, NJ: Princeton University Press, 2017.

Tetlock, Philip E., and Dan Gardner. *Superforecasting: The Art and Science of Prediction.* New York: Random House, 2016.

Turner, Marlene E., and Anthony R. Pratkanis. "Twenty-Five Years of Groupthink Theory and Research: Lessons from the Evaluation of a Theory." *Organizational Behavior and Human Decision Processes* 73, no. 2-3 (1998): 105-115.

Chapter 5

Butler, John, Douglas J. Morrice, and Peter W. Mullarkey. "A Multiple Attribute Utility Theory Approach to Ranking and Selection." *Management Science* 47, no. 6 (2001): 800-816.

Carroll, Paul, and Chunka Mui. *Billion Dollar Lessons: What You Can Learn from the Most Inexcusable Business Failures of the Last 25 Years*. New York: Penguin, 2008.

Gawande, Atul. *The Checklist Manifesto: How to Get Things Right*. New York: Henry Holt and Company, 2009.

Huber, George P. "Multi-Attribute Utility Models: A Review of Field and Field-Like Studies." *Management Science* 20, no. 10 (1974): 1393-1402.

Yang, Jian-Bo, and Dong-Ling Xu. "On the evidential reasoning algorithm for multiple attribute decision analysis under uncertainty." *IEEE Transactions on Systems, Man, and Cybernetics – Part A: Systems and Humans* 32, no. 3 (2002): 289-304.

Dr. Gleb Tsipursky Books

(co-written with Tim Ward) *Pro Truth: A Practical Plan for Putting Truth Back into Politics* **(Changemakers Books, 2020)**

How can we turn back the tide of post-truth politics, fake news, and misinformation that is damaging our democracy? First, by empowering citizens to recognize and resist political lies and deceptions: Using cutting-edge neuroscience research, we show you the tricks post-truth politicians use to exploit our mental blindspots and cognitive biases. We then share with you strategies to protect yourself and others from these threats. Second, by addressing the damage caused by the spread of fake news on social media: We provide you with effective techniques for fighting digital misinformation. Third, by exerting pressure on politicians, media, and other public figures: Doing so involves creating new incentives for telling the truth, new penalties for lying, and new ways of communicating across the partisan divide. To put this plan into action requires the rise of a Pro-Truth Movement – a movement which has already begun, and is making a tangible impact. If you believe truth matters, and want to protect our democracy, please read this book, and join us. Dr. Gleb Tsipursky and Tim Ward have teamed up to help citizens learn to protect themselves from lies, and empower them to put truth back into politics.

The Blindspots Between Us: How to Overcome Unconscious Cognitive Bias & Build Better Relationships **(New Harbinger, 2020)**

We all want positive, productive, and genuine relationships – whether it's with our co-workers, family, friends, peers, or romantic partners. And yet, time and time again, we all seem to make the same thinking errors that threaten or sabotage these relationships. These errors are called cognitive biases, and they happen when our brain attempts to simplify information by making assumptions. Grounded in evidence-based cognitive behavioral therapy (CBT), *The Blindspots Between Us* reveals the most common "hidden" cognitive biases that blind us to the truth, and which lead to the misunderstandings that damage our relationships. With this guide, you'll learn key skills to help you debias – to stop, pause, and objectively observe situations before jumping to conclusions about others' motives. You'll also learn to consider other people's points of view and past experiences before rushing to judgment and potentially undermining your relationships. Being human is hard. None of us are perfect, and we all have our blindspots that can get in the way of building the relationships we really and truly want, deep down. This much-needed book will help you identify your own mental blindspots, and move beyond them for better relationships – and a better world.

Never Go With Your Gut: How Pioneering Leaders Make the Best Decisions and Avoid Business Disasters (Career Press, 2019)

What brings down a business? Whether minor mishaps – like excessive team conflict, or major calamities – like those that threaten bankruptcy, nothing drives a business toward disaster as fast as poor decision-making. Behavioral economics and cognitive neuroscience studies reveal that our flawed mental patterns – what scholars call cognitive biases – trigger the poor decisions at the root of countless business disasters. And that traditional advice to "go with your gut" is actually a strategic error that costs organizations and careers. Combining practical case studies with cutting-edge research, leadership and decision-making expert Dr. Gleb Tsipursky debunks the myth of leading by instinct and provides powerful tactics to avoid business disasters in his new book. It's the first book to focus on cognitive biases in business leadership, revealing how we can overcome these dangerous judgment errors effectively, and revealing the counterintuitive secret to the success of pioneering leaders and organizations. *Never Go With Your Gut* shows leaders how to improve their business decision-making in easy but essential steps, relying on data and evidence over emotions. It builds a practical framework for dismantling the traps of bias, bad advice and skewed judgment. Filled with real-world examples and compelling research, the book exposes the limitations of leading on instinct, empowering leaders of any organization to make the decisions that sustain success.

Find Your Purpose Using Science (Intentional Insights, 2015)

This workbook helps you live a meaningful life by finding and living your purpose using science-based strategies. It combines an engaging narrative, stories from people's lives, and research-informed exercises and worksheets designed to help you cultivate a rich sense of meaning and purpose. Written by Dr. Gleb Tsipursky, this workbook draws on the author's scholarship on meaning and purpose and his experience as a science popularizer. Science really can answer life's big questions, such as "why am I here," as shown by a wave of recent research in psychology, cognitive neuroscience, and medicine. The research highlights that such questions are vital, since people who lack a rich sense of purpose have significantly worse mental and physical health. The vast majority of guidance on meaning and purpose comes from traditional sources such as cultural heritage and religion. While this guidance works for some, unfortunately traditional sources of meaning and purpose do not speak nearly so well to others who want an evidence-based approach in which they can be truly confident. This workbook offers science-based strategies and data-driven tools to help you improve your mental and physical health by finding the meaning of your life and thus living with a purpose. Read this book to find your purpose using science!

The Truth-Seeker's Handbook: A Science-Based Guide (Intentional Insights, 2017)

How do you know whether something is true? How do you convince others to believe the facts? Research in cognitive neuroscience and behavioral economics shows that we often make dangerous judgment errors, what scholars call cognitive biases. These mental blindspots cause us to believe comfortable lies over inconvenient truths. Such errors leave us vulnerable to making the wrong decisions based on false beliefs. These poor choices lead to disastrous consequences for our business, personal lives, relationships, and civic engagement. Fortunately, scientists have uncovered many useful strategies for overcoming our mental flaws. *The Truth-Seeker's Handbook* presents a variety of research-based tools for ensuring that our beliefs are aligned with reality. With examples from daily life and an engaging style, *The Truth-Seeker's Handbook* will provide you with the skills to avoid cognitive biases and help others to do so. Using these strategies, you will prevent disasters and maximize success for yourself, those you care about, your organization, and our society.

Dr. Gleb Tsipursky Bio

Known as the Disaster Avoidance Expert, Dr. Gleb Tsipursky is an internationally-recognized thought leader on a mission to protect leaders from dangerous judgment errors known as cognitive biases, which devastate bottom lines and bring down high-flying careers. His expertise and passion is developing the most effective and profitable decision-making strategies, based on pragmatic business experience and cutting-edge behavioral economics and cognitive neuroscience, to empower leaders to avoid business disasters and maximize their bottom lines. You can learn more here: https://disasteravoidanceexperts.com/glebtsipursky/.

The bestselling author of several books, Dr. Tsipursky is best known for his national best-seller *Never Go With Your Gut: How Pioneering Leaders Make the Best Decisions and Avoid Business Disasters* (Career Press, 2019), the first book to focus on cognitive biases in business leadership and reveal how leaders can overcome these dangerous judgment errors effectively. He also published a book on seeing the truth of reality to defeat dangerous judgment errors, *The Truth-Seeker's Handbook: A Science-Based Guide* (Intentional Insights, 2017). His newest published book is *The Blindspots Between Us: How to Overcome Unconscious Cognitive Bias and Build Better Relationships* (New Harbinger, April 2020), the first book to focus on cognitive biases in professional and personal relationships and illustrate how we can defeat these dangerous judgment errors in our relationships. His new book is *Resilience: Adapt and Plan for the New Abnormal of the COVID-19 Coronavirus Pandemic* (Changemakers Books, 2020). It helps organizations and individuals navigate successfully the major disruption of the COVID-19 coronavirus pandemic and succeed in the post-pandemic world. See more information here: https://disasteravoidanceexperts.com/author-page/.

Dr. Tsipursky's cutting-edge thought leadership was featured in over 550 articles he published and over 450 interviews he gave to popular venues that include *Fast Company*, *Entrepreneur*, *CBS News*, *Time*, *Scientific American*, *Psychology Today*, *The Conversation*, *Business Insider*, *Government Executive*, *The Chronicle of Philanthropy*, *Inc. Magazine*, and many others, as you can see here, https://disasteravoidanceexperts.com/media/.

Dr. Tsipursky's expertise comes from over 20 years of consulting, coaching, speaking, and training for businesses and nonprofits. He serves as the CEO of the boutique consulting, coaching, and training firm Disaster Avoidance Experts, which uses a proprietary methodology based on groundbreaking research to help leaders and organizations maximize their bottom lines by addressing potential threats, seizing unexpected opportunities, and resolving persistent personnel problems. His clients include Aflac, Balance Employment Assistance Provider, Edison Welding Institute, Fifth Third Bank, Honda, International Coach Federation, Ohio Hospital Association, National Association of Women Business Owners, Sentinel Real Estate, The Society for Human Resource Management, RealManage, The Columbus Foundation, Vistage, Wells Fargo, the World Wildlife Fund, Xerox, and over a hundred others who achieve outstanding client results. You can learn more about that here: https://disasteravoidanceexperts.com/about.

His expertise also comes from his research and teaching background as a behavioral economist and cognitive neuroscientist studying the psychology of decision-making in business and other contexts. He spent over 15 years in academia, including seven years as a professor at The Ohio State University and before that as a Fellow at the University of North Carolina-Chapel Hill. His dozens of peer-reviewed academic publications have appeared in well-respected scholarly journals such as *Behavior and Social Issues*, *Journal of Social and Political Psychology*, and *International Journal of Existential Psychology and*

Psychotherapy.

His civic service includes over four years as the Chair of the Board of Directors of Intentional Insights, an educational nonprofit advocating for research-based decision-making in all life areas. He also co-founded the Pro-Truth Pledge, a civic project to promote truthfulness and integrity for individual professionals and leaders in the same way that the Better Business Bureau serves as a commitment for businesses. He serves on the Advisory Board of Canonical Debate Lab and Planet Purpose, and is on the Editorial Board of the peer-reviewed journal *Behavior and Social Issues.*

A highly in-demand international speaker, Dr. Tsipursky has over two decades of professional speaking experience across North America, Europe, and Australia. He gets top marks from audiences for his highly facilitative, interactive, and humor-filled speaking style and the way he thoroughly customizes speeches for diverse audiences. Meeting planners describe Dr. Tsipursky as "very relatable," as "a snap to work with," and as someone who "does everything that you would want a speaker to do." Drawing on best practices in adult learning, his programs address the wide spectrum of diverse learning styles, as attested by enthusiastic client testimonials and references. He regularly shares the stage with prominent leaders, for example recently speaking on a roundtable panel with the President of the European Commission Ursula von der Leyen, Secretary General of the International Federation of Red Cross and Red Crescent Societies Elhadj As Sy, Chancellor of Austria Brigitte Bierlein, CEO of Penguin Random House Markus Dohle, and billionaire philanthropist and Chair of the Bertelsmann Management Company Liz Mohn. You can learn more about his speaking and see videos here: https://disasteravoidanceexperts. com/speaking/.

Dr. Tsipursky earned his PhD in the History of Behavioral Science at the University of North Carolina at Chapel Hill in

2011, his MA at Harvard University in 2004, and his BA at New York University in 2002. He lives in and travels from Columbus, OH. In his free time, he enjoys tennis, hiking, and playing with his two cats, and most importantly, he makes sure to spend abundant quality time with his wife to avoid disasters in his personal life.

Learn more about him at https://DisasterAvoidanceExperts.com/GlebTsipursky, contact him at:

Gleb@DisasterAvoidanceExperts.com,
follow him on Instagram @dr_gleb_tsipursky
and Twitter @gleb_tsipursky. Most importantly, help yourself
avoid disasters and maximize success, and get a free copy of
Assessment on Dangerous Judgment Errors in the Workplace, by
signing up for his free Wise Decision Maker Course at:
https://DisasterAvoidanceExperts.com/Subscribe.

TRANSFORMATION

The *Resilience* Series

The Resilience Series is a collaborative effort by the authors of Changemakers Books in response to the 2020 coronavirus epidemic. Each concise volume offers expert advice and practical exercises for mastering specific skills and abilities. Our intention is that by strengthening your resilience, you can better survive and even thrive in a time of crisis.

Resilience: Adapt and Plan for the New Abnormal of the COVID-19 Coronavirus Pandemic
by Gleb Tsipursky

COVID-19 has demonstrated clearly that businesses, nonprofits, individuals, and governments are terrible at dealing effectively with large-scale disasters that take the form of slow-moving train-wrecks. Using cutting-edge research in cognitive neuroscience and behavioral economics on dangerous judgment errors (cognitive biases), this book first explains why we respond so poorly to slow-moving, high-impact, and long-term crises. Next, the book shares research-based strategies for how organizations and individuals can adapt effectively to the new abnormal of the COVID-19 pandemic and similar disasters. Finally, it shows how to develop an effective strategic plan and make the best major decisions in the context of the uncertainty and ambiguity brought about by COVID-19 and other slow-moving large-scale catastrophes. The author, a cognitive neuroscientist and behavioral economist and CEO of the consulting, coaching, and training firm Disaster Avoidance Experts, combines research-based strategies with real-life stories from his business and nonprofit clients as they adapt to the pandemic.

Resilience: Aging with Vision, Hope and Courage in a Time of Crisis
by John C. Robinson

This book is for those over 65 wrestling with fear, despair, insecurity, and loneliness in these frightening times. A blend of psychology, self-help, and spirituality, it's meant for all who hunger for facts, respect, compassion, and meaningful resources to light their path ahead. The 74-year-old author's goal is to move readers from fear and paralysis to growth and engagement: "Acknowledging the inspiring resilience and wisdom of our hard-won maturity, I invite you on a personal journey of transformation and renewal into a new consciousness and a new world."

Resilience: Connecting with Nature in a Time of Crisis
by Melanie Choukas-Bradley

Nature is one of the best medicines for difficult times. An intimate awareness of the natural world, even within the city, can calm anxieties and help create healthy perspectives. This book will inspire and guide you as you deal with the current crisis, or any personal or worldly distress. The author is a naturalist and certified forest therapy guide who leads nature and forest bathing walks for many organizations in Washington, DC and the American West. Learn from her the Japanese art of "forest bathing": how to tune in to the beauty and wonder around you with all your senses, even if your current sphere is a tree outside the window or a wild backyard. Discover how you can become a backyard naturalist, learning about the trees, wildflowers, birds and animals near your home. Nature immersion during stressful times can bring comfort and joy as well as opportunities for personal growth, expanded vision and transformation.

Resilience: Going Within in a Time of Crisis
by P.T. Mistlberger

During a time of crisis, we are presented with something of a fork in the road; we either look within and examine ourselves, or engage in distractions and go back to sleep. This book is intended to be a companion for men and women dedicated to their inner journey. Written by the author of seven books and founder of several personal growth communities and esoteric schools, each chapter offers different paths for exploring your spiritual frontier: advanced meditation techniques, shadow work, conscious relating, dream work, solo retreats, and more. In traversing these challenging times, let this book be your guide.

Resilience: Grow Stronger in a Time of Crisis
by Linda Ferguson

Many of us have wondered how we would respond in the midst of a crisis. You hope that difficult times could bring out the best in you. Some become stronger, more resilient and more innovative under pressure. You hope that you will too. But you are afraid that crisis may bring out your anxiety, your fears and your weakest communication. No one knows when the crisis will pass and things will get better. That's out of your hands. But *you* can get better. All it takes is an understanding of how human beings function at their best, the willpower to make small changes in perception and behavior, and a vision of a future that is better than today. In the pages of this book, you will learn to create the conditions that allow your best self to show up and make a difference – for you and for others.

Resilience: Handling Anxiety in a Time of Crisis
by George Hofmann

It's a challenging time for people who experience anxiety, and even people who usually don't experience it are finding their moods are getting the better of them. Anxiety hits hard and its symptoms are unmistakable, but sometimes in the rush and confusion of uncertainty we miss those symptoms until it's too late. When things seem to be coming undone, it's still possible to recognize the onset of anxiety and act to prevent the worst of it. The simple steps taught in this book can help you overcome the turmoil.

Resilience: The Life-Saving Skill of Story
by Michelle Auerbach

Storytelling covers every skill we need in a crisis. We need to share information about how to be safe, about how to live together, about what to do and not do. We need to talk about what is going on in ways that keep us from freaking out. We need to change our behavior as a human race to save each other and ourselves. We need to imagine a possible future different from the present and work on how to get there. And we need to do it all without falling apart. This book will help people in any field and any walk of life to become better storytellers and immediately unleash the power to teach, learn, change, soothe, and create community to activate ourselves and the people around us.

Resilience: Navigating Loss in a Time of Crisis
by Jules De Vitto

This book explores the many forms of loss that can happen in times of crisis. These losses can range from loss of business, financial security, routine, structure to the deeper losses of meaning, purpose or identity. The author draws on her background in transpersonal psychology, integrating spiritual insights and mindfulness practices to take the reader on a journey in which to help them navigate the stages of uncertainty that follow loss. The book provides several practical activities, guided visualization and meditations to cultivate greater resilience, courage and strength and also explores the potential to find greater meaning and purpose through times of crisis.

Resilience: Virtually Speaking
Communicating at a Distance
by Teresa Erickson and Tim Ward

To adapt to a world where you can't meet face-to-face – with air travel and conferences cancelled, teams working from home – leaders, experts, managers and professionals all need to master the skills of virtual communication. Written by the authors of *The Master Communicator's Handbook*, this book tells you how to create impact with your on-screen presence, use powerful language to motivate listening, and design compelling visuals. You will also learn techniques to prevent your audience from losing attention, to keep them engaged from start to finish, and to create a lasting impact.

Resilience: Virtual Teams
Holding the Center When You Can't Meet Face-to-Face
by Carlos Valdes-Dapena

In the face of the COVID-19 virus organizations large and small are shuttering offices and factories, requiring as much work as possible be done from people's homes. The book draws on the insights of the author's earlier book, *Lessons from Mars,* providing a set of the powerful tools and exercises developed within the

Mars Corporation to create high performance teams. These tools have been adapted for teams suddenly forced to work apart, in many cases for the first time. These simple secrets and tested techniques have been used by thousands of teams who know that creating a foundation of team identity and shared meaning makes them resilient, even in a time of crisis.